Inspired Wire

Inspired Wire

Learn to twist, jig, bend, hammer, and wrap wire for the prettiest jewelry ever

CYNTHIA B. WULLER

KALMBACH BOOKS

Contents

© 2008 Cynthia B. Wuller. All rights reserved. This book may not be reproduced in part or in whole without written permission of the publisher, except in the case of brief quotations used in reviews. Published by Kalmbach Publishing Co., 21027 Crossroads Circle, Waukesha, WI 53186.

Printed in the United States of America

14 13 12 11 10   3 4 5 6 7

The jewelry designs in *Inspired Wire* are copyrighted. Please use them for your education and personal enjoyment only. They may not be taught or sold without permission.

Publisher's Cataloging-In-Publication Data

Wuller, Cynthia B.
  Inspired wire : learn to twist, jig, bend, hammer, and wrap wire for the prettiest jewelry ever / Cynthia B. Wuller.

    p. : col. ill. ; cm.

  ISBN: 978-0-87116-256-4

1. Jewelry making--Handbooks, manuals, etc. 2. Wire jewelry--Handbooks, manuals, etc. 3. Wire jewelry--Patterns.

TT212 .W85 2008
745.594/2

Cold-connection wire jewelry appeals to me because I can make pieces at home with a few tools and supplies, and very little mess. I also love the almost instant gratification of creating this jewelry. I am known to whip up baubles (frantically) minutes before leaving the house, testing my husband's patience. At the same time, it's great to put my stamp on what I wear.

My work is inspired by women in fairy tales, folk tales, and mythology. They have entertained me since childhood and come alive through my jewelry. I also design pieces to test new techniques, and I make things that I want to wear.

My background is rooted in drawing, fashion design, fiber art, and, of course, jewelry design and metal working. I combine techniques, ideas, and tools from these different areas to create my pieces.

When conceptualizing designs and ideas, I sketch, play with wire, and drape links on a necklace bust to check flow and movement. I find it very important to step away from the piece and look at it while it's draped – from all angles and in a mirror. For the best aesthetic appeal, it's necessary to make sure any jewelry looks good from every direction. Sometimes I can envision the end product, and other times I let the materials guide me.

I wrote this book to teach my techniques and designs. The projects build on each other, so if you start from the beginning, you'll be able to complete the projects at the end. If you are new to wire working, it's best to start from the very beginning. If you have experience and want to jump around the book, please take the time to familiarize yourself with Chapter 1; I do the basics a little differently than other designers.

You might find that the projects at the end of a chapter are too difficult; in that case, go on to the next chapter's beginner projects. Then return and try those challenging pieces again. You'll most likely be able to complete them. Challenging projects can be very satisfying. You'll gain technique and confidence, and a great piece of jewelry is your reward.

All of the jewelry in this book fits me, since I'm the only model I have. If you need a different size, add or take away an extra link or a bead or two for a better fit; just try to keep the piece symmetrical.

This book has five chapters. Chapter 1 is all about the basics – techniques, links, and clasps – used throughout the book, and is a reference for the rest of the projects. Chapter 2 mixes the basics with pre-made chain and findings to incorporate and practice the skills you've just learned. Chapter 3 is all about using a jig, including a lot of wire manipulation, such as hammering and reshaping links. Chapter 4 introduces shaping on objects such as a ring mandrel and a pen barrel. And, the shaping in Chapter 5 is with only your hands and your pliers. A good understanding of the previous chapters is needed to complete these more complicated projects.

Wire is a fun and easy material to work with. Think of it as a line that can be made into two-dimensional and three-dimensional shapes. Learning the right techniques will make the wire react the way you want it to. Once you understand wire's qualities, making jewelry becomes fun and easy. At the same time, its easy malleability also leads to unwanted kinks or bends. The best advice I can give is to make sure to remove those imperfections. Clamp the wire in your chain-nose pliers and gently squeeze the kinks to remove them. Do this after every step for a flawless looking piece.

The focus of my jewelry is not the beads; it is the wire, the process, and the techniques. That being said, the beads are not an afterthought. They are an integral part of the pieces, adding embellishment, color, and texture. I use semi-precious stones and pearls because those materials bring a natural glow to the pieces. They cost a little bit more, but the elegance they add is priceless.

Craft wire is my preference. In a way, it's a cheap thrill, but I get a kick out of transforming a base material into a piece of jewelry that looks so lavish. Each project can be made with craft wire or precious metal. I strongly suggest you try them first with craft wire. Many projects look simple, but the processes can be quite tricky. It's always better on your pocketbook to practice first.

Thank you for giving my book a try. I hope you enjoy the results!

Cynthia B. Wuller

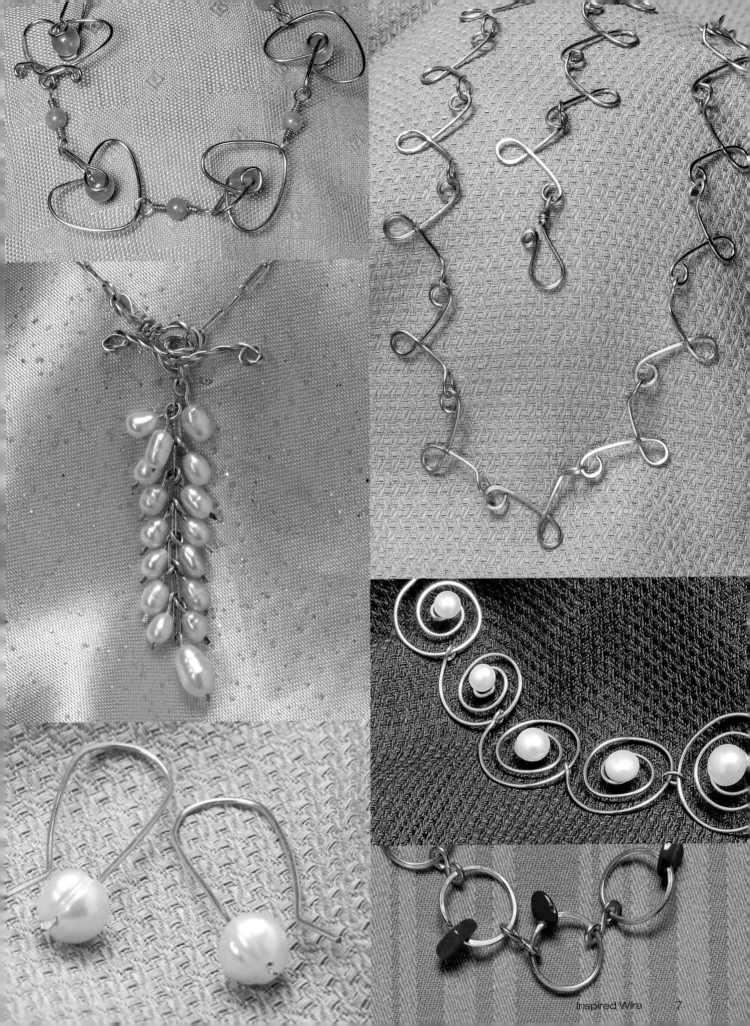

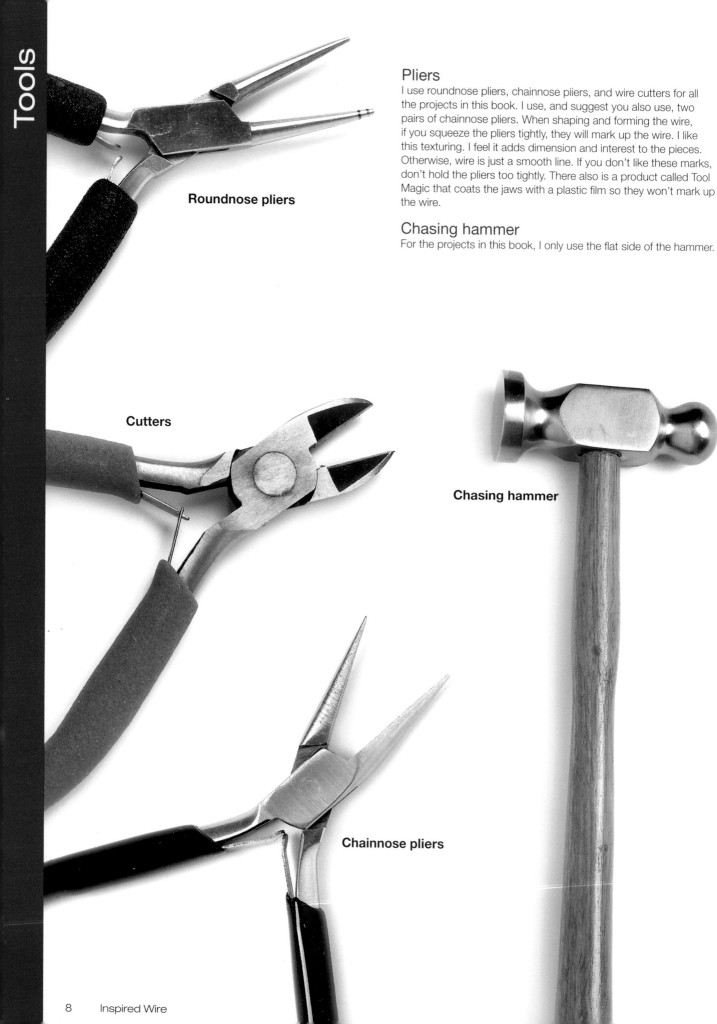

Roundnose pliers

Pliers

I use roundnose pliers, chainnose pliers, and wire cutters for all the projects in this book. I use, and suggest you also use, two pairs of chainnose pliers. When shaping and forming the wire, if you squeeze the pliers tightly, they will mark up the wire. I like this texturing. I feel it adds dimension and interest to the pieces. Otherwise, wire is just a smooth line. If you don't like these marks, don't hold the pliers too tightly. There also is a product called Tool Magic that coats the jaws with a plastic film so they won't mark up the wire.

Chasing hammer

For the projects in this book, I only use the flat side of the hammer.

Cutters

Chasing hammer

Chainnose pliers

Ruler

The C-Thru ruler is very handy because of the grid. I use two sizes: 8ths Graph Beveled ruler in 2 in. x 18 in. and 1 in. x 6 in.

Dapping or bench block

The pieces and links are hammered on this steel block. It's a little expensive compared to the other tools, but I use mine often.

Vise

I picked mine up at the local hardware store. It has a suction bottom and two rubber protectors for the jaw of the vise (which I did not use for the projects in this book). I love how it's portable. Any vise will do, as long as it is sturdy and large enough to hold a ring mandrel while it's being hammered. For a tight suction hold, I use a smooth, hardcover book as a base because my work table is uneven.

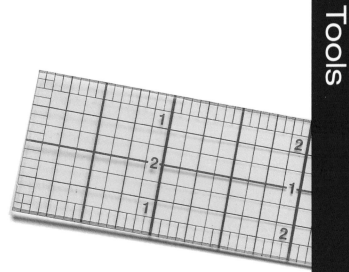

C-Thru ruler

Bench block

Vise

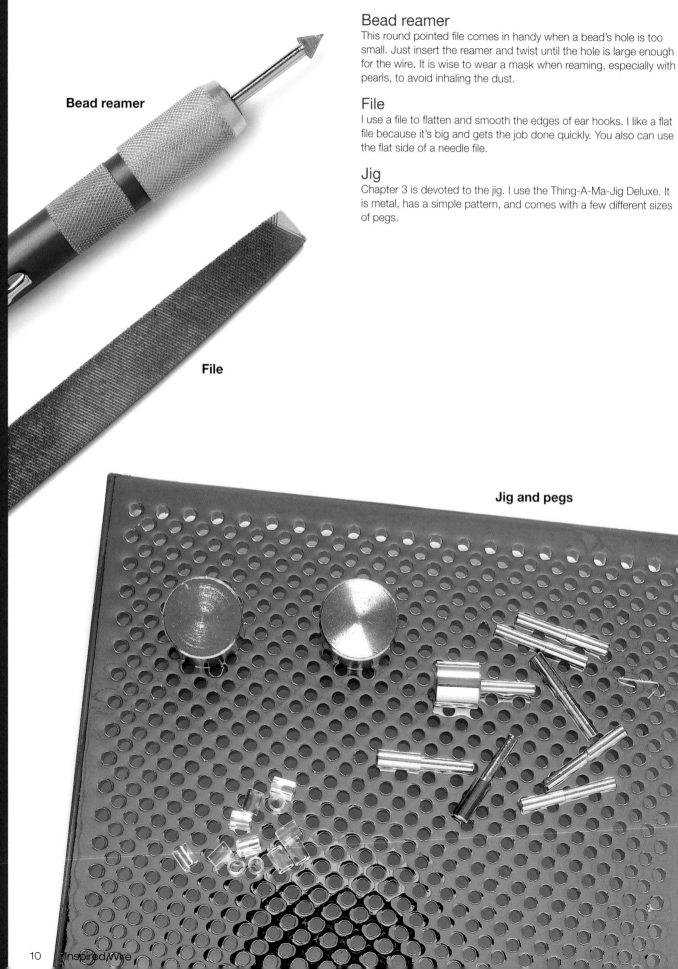

Bead reamer

File

Jig and pegs

Bead reamer
This round pointed file comes in handy when a bead's hole is too small. Just insert the reamer and twist until the hole is large enough for the wire. It is wise to wear a mask when reaming, especially with pearls, to avoid inhaling the dust.

File
I use a file to flatten and smooth the edges of ear hooks. I like a flat file because it's big and gets the job done quickly. You also can use the flat side of a needle file.

Jig
Chapter 3 is devoted to the jig. I use the Thing-A-Ma-Jig Deluxe. It is metal, has a simple pattern, and comes with a few different sizes of pegs.

Mandrels

I use two: a metal ring mandrel and a pen (see below). For the projects in chapter 4, Form Shaping Links, you must have a metal ring mandrel because a lot of hammering is done directly on the mandrel. It is a good investment if you like to make rings and ring shapes. Secure a mandrel in a vise.

Pen

The Sharpie Ultra Fine Point does triple duty. It's used to mark the roundnose pliers for loop guides, as a form for ear hooks and clasp hooks in a few projects, and as a mandrel.

Adhesive

Two types of glue are used in projects in this book. (Both have their advantages and disadvantages, so use the glue called for in the instructions.) Loctite 454 dries quickly. G-S Hypo Cement takes about 10 minutes to dry, so there is more give when putting a project together. I like to let my glued pieces cure for a few hours or overnight. If the pieces are still loose after that, which can happen with G-S Hypo Cement, re-apply the glue and let it cure. Once securely glued, both form a strong bond. Common cyanoacrylate glue is an acceptable substitute for Loctite 454. It's not as strong, but it isn't as tough on your skin if you accidentally get some on your hands. I wear a mask when gluing.

Wrist support

The repetitive motion of wire-jewelry making can cause your wrists to be sore, or worse. I wear carpal-tunnel wrist supports made by Mueller; buy these in any drug store. It's also a good idea to do stretching exercises every hour for your wrists and your whole body. Proper working posture is good, too. Try to keep what you're working on at eye level and don't hunch over. If something hurts, stop and rest.

Metal ring mandrel

Pen

Adhesive

Adhesive

Wrist support

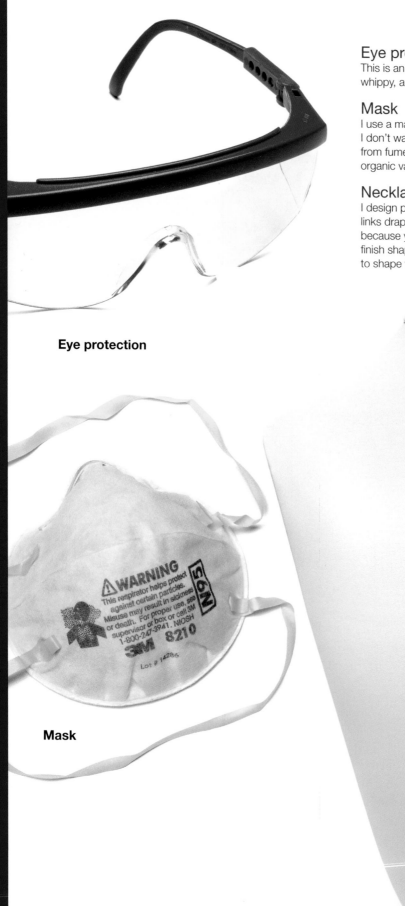

Eye protection

Mask

Necklace bust

Eye protection

This is an absolute must for every project at all times. Wire is quite whippy, and tools slip. It's better to be protected.

Mask

I use a mask whenever there's a chance I could be inhaling things I don't want in my lungs – bead dust in particular. For protection from fumes, request a particulate respirator with nuisance-level organic vapor relief (for example, 3M 8577, not shown).

Necklace bust

I design pieces on a 14-in. velvet necklace bust. I prefer to see how links drape on the form when designing. Velvet busts are good because you can pin into them. A few projects require a bust to finish shaping the pieces. If you don't want to get one, you can try to shape the piece on yourself or a friend.

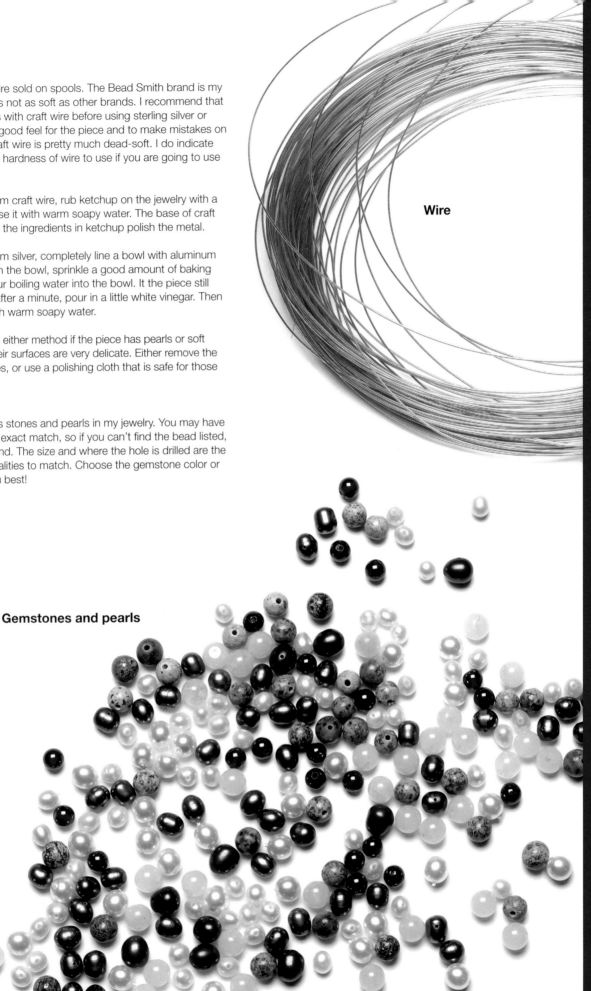

Wire

I like to use craft wire sold on spools. The Bead Smith brand is my favorite because it's not as soft as other brands. I recommend that you try the projects with craft wire before using sterling silver or gold-filled to get a good feel for the piece and to make mistakes on the cheap wire. Craft wire is pretty much dead-soft. I do indicate in every project the hardness of wire to use if you are going to use precious metal.

To clean tarnish from craft wire, rub ketchup on the jewelry with a soft cloth. Then rinse it with warm soapy water. The base of craft wire is copper, and the ingredients in ketchup polish the metal.

To clean tarnish from silver, completely line a bowl with aluminum foil. Put the piece in the bowl, sprinkle a good amount of baking soda on it, and pour boiling water into the bowl. It the piece still has some tarnish after a minute, pour in a little white vinegar. Then wash the piece with warm soapy water.

I don't recommend either method if the piece has pearls or soft stones because their surfaces are very delicate. Either remove the pearls or soft stones, or use a polishing cloth that is safe for those materials.

Beads

I use semi-precious stones and pearls in my jewelry. You may have difficulty finding an exact match, so if you can't find the bead listed, look for a similar kind. The size and where the hole is drilled are the most important qualities to match. Choose the gemstone color or finish that suits you best!

Wire

Gemstones and pearls

The Basics

This chapter really is the beginning. It contains all of the techniques and basics used to make the projects in the following chapters. Practice all of the projects in this chapter. You need a good understanding of these basics to complete the following, more advanced, projects. You'll refer back to this chapter throughout the book.

You'll find the *Quick Measurement Guide* on page 17. Use this when you've memorized how to make the basics, but can't remember the specifics. I refer to it quite often. Make a photocopy of the guide to keep next to you so you won't have to flip through the book to find it.

When a project calls for a jump ring, clasp, bead link, or anything else covered in Basics, you'll see it listed in the Make Ahead Ⓒ list that follows the Materials list, along with a page reference to this chapter.

MARKING ROUNDNOSE PLIERS

Marking your pliers is a good way to keep your loops symmetrical. As we progress through the book, you'll find the project directions specify which mark to use in order to make a correctly sized loop based on the wire you're using. Later, when we begin to use the jig, we'll add markings to the pliers. I color-code my marks to avoid confusion.

We'll begin with two marks, Mark 1 and Mark 2. Generally, Mark 1 is for thinner 22- and 24-gauge wire. Mark 2 is for thicker 20-gauge wire. Twisted wire is usually formed on Mark 2, since it is thick.

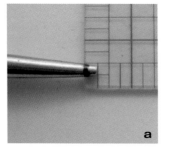

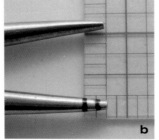

Tools
- roundnose pliers
- fine-tip black permanent marker
- ruler

TIP: These markings will rub as you use your pliers, so re-mark them as needed.

Mark 1
Use a ruler to measure in 1/16 in. (1.5mm) on one jaw of your roundnose pliers. Mark that spot with the marker, drawing a circle around the entire jaw **a**.

Mark 2
Make a second mark on the same jaw of the roundnose pliers, 1/8 in. (3mm) in from the tip **b**.

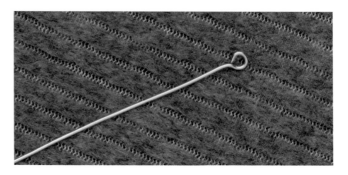

STRAIGHTENING A LOOP
Straightening a loop gives it a finished look, makes it sturdier, and makes it easier to open and close.

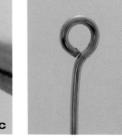

Materials
- 20-gauge wire

Tools
- roundnose pliers

Grasp the tip of a piece of wire on Mark 2 of your roundnose pliers. Roll the wire with the pliers to make a loop **a**.

With the tip of your roundnose pliers, gently pinch the loop at the base **b**.

Center the loop on the wire by turning it away from you slightly so it looks like a lollipop **c, d**.

QUICK MEASUREMENT GUIDE

	Finding	22- or 24-gauge Wire	20-gauge Wire
	S-link	Form loops on Mark 1; cut wire for second loop at ¼ in. (6.5mm)	Form loops on Mark 2; cut wire for second loop at ¼ in. (6.5mm)
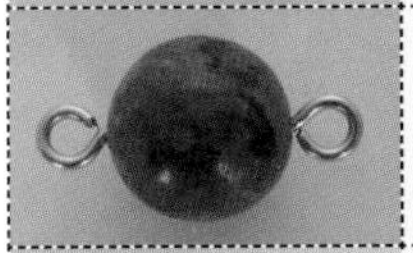	Bead link	Form first loop on Mark 1 and second loop at 5/16 in. (8mm)	Form first loop on Mark 2 and second loop at 3/8 in. (9.5mm)
	Wrapped loop bead link	Form loops on Mark 1 with the first loop at 5/8 in. (16mm) and the second at ¾ in. (19mm)	Form loops on Mark 2 with the first loop at ¾ in. (19mm) and the second at 7/8 in. (22mm)
	Headpin	Cut wire 5/16 in. (8mm) above the bead and form loop on Mark 1	Cut wire 3/8 in. (9.5mm) above the bead and form loop on Mark 2
	Wrapped loop headpin	Cut wire 5/8 in. (16mm) above the bead and form loop on Mark 1	Cut wire ¾ in. (19mm) above the bead and form loop on Mark 2
	Eye	Cut wire ¾ in. (19mm) and form loop on Mark 1 halfway down roundnose pliers	Cut wire 1 in. (25.5mm) and form loop on Mark 2 ¾ of the way down round-nose pliers
	Wrapped loop eye	Cut wire 1½ in. (38mm) and form loop around the base of roundnose pliers	Cut wire 1¾ in. (44mm) and form loop around the base of roundnose pliers
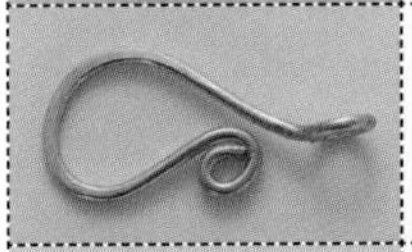	Hook	Cut wire 1½ in. (38mm) and form loop on Mark 1	Cut wire 1¾ in. (44mm) and form loop on Mark 2
	Wrapped loop hook	Cut wire 2 in. (51mm) and form loop on Mark 2 at 5/8 in. (16mm)	Cut wire 2¼ in. (57mm) and form loop on Mark 2 at ¾ in. (19mm)
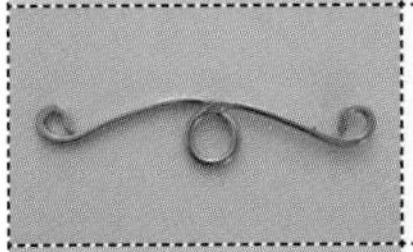	Toggle	(don't use 22- or 24-gauge wire)	Cut wire 2 in. (51mm) and form center loop one-third of the way down roundnose pliers
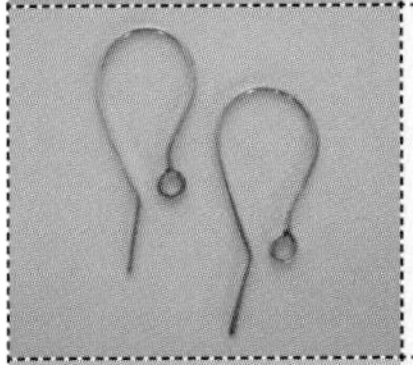	Ear hooks	Cut wires 2 in. (51mm) and form loops on Mark 1	Cut wires 2 in. (51mm) and form loops on Mark 2
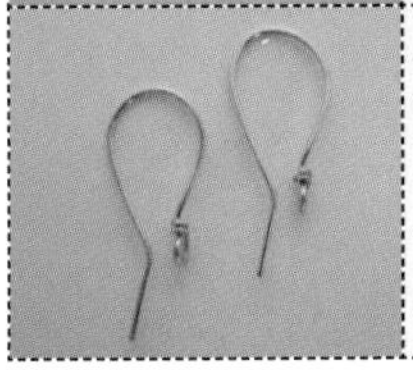	Wrapped loop ear hooks	Cut wires 2¼ in. (57mm) and form wrapped loop at ½ in. (13mm)	Cut wires 2¼ in. (57mm) and form wrapped loop at ½ in. (13mm)

HAMMERING

The benefits of hammering are twofold: They are practical, because the wire becomes work hardened, and they are aesthetic, because the wire gains texture and becomes flat. Hammering techniques add stability and character to wire pieces. Hold the hammer toward the base of the handle and use your elbow (not your wrist) to hammer.

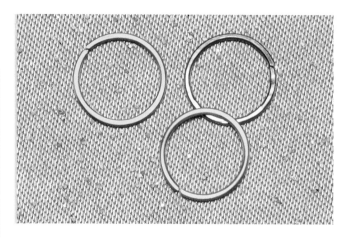

Un-hammered link	**Work-hardened link**

Flattened link	**Textured link**

a

b

c

d

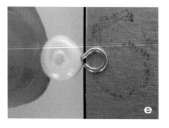

e

f

Materials
• wire or wire link

Tools
• chasing hammer
• bench block

Work harden

Wire is quite malleable. To make it stronger, it can be gently hammered. Put the link on the block **a**. Lightly tap the link with your hammer a few times **b**. Be sure to hammer straight down, with the head parallel to the block, to avoid putting nicks in the link. If a link is large or loses its shape when hammering, press part of it to the block with your finger and hammer. Turn the link and lightly hammer the side you were pressing with your finger. Flip the link over and lightly hammer the back. The wire gets slightly flattened. Hammering to work harden helps the link hold its shape.

Flatten

Keep the face of the hammer parallel with the block as when work hardening **b**. To get wire or a link flat, hammer the piece on the block harder and a few more times than when work hardening. Turn over and repeat on the other side. Hammer just until the wire is almost completely flat (but not distorted). The edge of the wire should still be slightly rounded, and the hammered wire will be much wider. If you hammer too much, the wire will become thin and break. Flattening really changes the feel of wire.

Texture

To add texture to a link, bring the hammer down at a slight angle so the edge hits the link **c**. If a link is large or it loses its shape when hammering, press part of it to the block with your finger and hammer **d**. Turn over and repeat on the other side. I love to texture wire. All of the nicks and hammer marks add more spots for light to reflect, causing a sparkle effect. If you like both textured and smooth surfaces, you should have two bench blocks and hammers, one specifically for creating texture and one for everything else. The block will get some nicks and scratches from texture hammering that could mar another piece.

Avoiding beads and wrapped sections

Put the link loop on the block with the bead or the wrapped section off over the side **e**. With your thumbnail or index fingernail, cover the bead or wrapped section to protect it while hammering **f**.

TWISTING WIRE IN A VISE
Twisting adds a different textural element to wire.

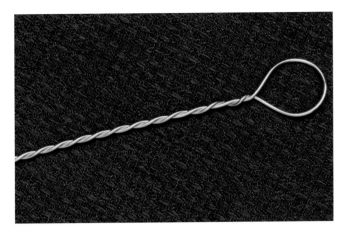

Materials
• dead-soft wire:
  20 gauge,
  22 gauge, or
  24 gauge

Tools
• chainnose pliers
• pen
• vise
• cutters

Each project will specify the length of wire needed. To practice, cut a 20-in. (50.8cm) length of wire.

Bring the ends of the wire together. Grasp the ends with chainnose pliers and twist the wires away from you a few times, forming a twist about ½ in. (13mm) long **a**.

Clamp part of the twisted wire in the vise **b**. Slip the pen into the center of the wire **c**, and keeping the wire taut, twist it away from you until it begins to kink or the twisted wire is the desired length, as called for in project instructions **d**.

With chainnose pliers, twist and pinch the ends of the wire together if they separated **e**.

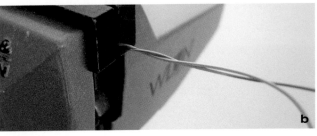

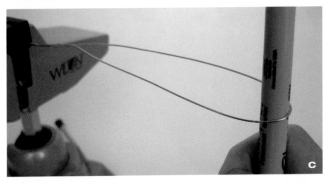

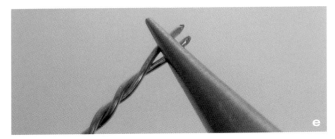

JUMP RINGS

This is the easiest way to make jump rings using only pliers.

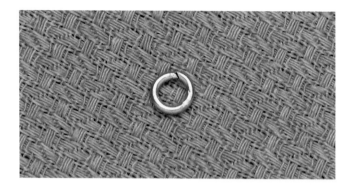

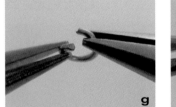

Materials
• 20- or 22-gauge dead-soft or half-hard wire

Tools
• 2 pairs of chainnose pliers
• roundnose pliers
• cutters

Form the coil
Tightly wrap the wire around one jaw of your roundnose pliers using short motions with your hand **a**. As you work, move the spiral toward you so the next wrap is formed in the same spot on the plier's jaw to keep the spiral the same diameter **b**. Each complete wrap on the spiral makes one ring. Wrap enough wire to make as many rings as you need **c**.

Cut the rings
Cut the rings from the spiral at a slight angle, so the rings close with a tight fit **d, e**. When cutting jump rings, I prefer to hold my cutters upside down so I can better see where I am cutting – but do what works best for you.

Open and close jump rings
Hold a jump ring with two pairs of chainnose pliers so the opening is centered between the pliers, as shown **f**. Push one pair of pliers away from you to open the ring **g**. Bring the same pair of pliers back toward you to close the ring **h**.

S-LINK

This simple S- or figure-8 shaped link is quite useful for connecting bead links or more elaborate wire links without distracting from the overall design.

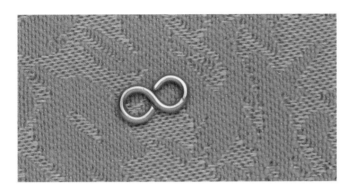

Materials
• 20- or 22-gauge dead-soft or half-hard wire

Tools
• 2 pairs of chainnose pliers
• roundnose pliers
• cutters
• ruler

Form the first link loop

On a spool of wire, form a loop (use Mark 1 for 22-gauge wire and Mark 2 for 20-gauge wire), rolling the tip of the wire away from you with roundnose pliers. Don't straighten the loop.

Trim the wire, leaving a ¼-in. (6.5mm) tail under the loop **a**.

Form the second link loop

Hold the loop with chainnose pliers with the wire end pointing toward you **b**, and form a second loop with roundnose pliers as you did the first **c, d**. Adjust the link as necessary so it's symmetrical **e**.

Opening and closing the link

To open the link, firmly hold each loop in a pair of chainnose pliers as shown. Using the second pair of chainnose pliers, push the tip of the pliers away from you to open the loop **f**.

Close the link by bringing the jaw of the chainnose pliers back toward you. Reshape the link as needed.

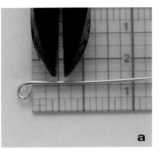
a

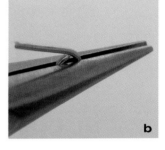
b

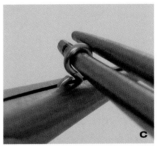
c

d

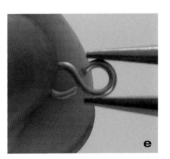
e

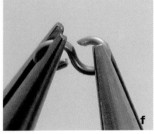
f

Basics

BEAD LINK

A bead link is a basic link usually used as a connector or to form chains.

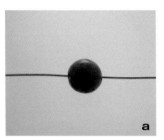

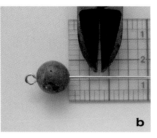

Materials
- 20- or 22-gauge dead-soft or half-hard wire (24 gauge is too flimsy)
- bead

Tools
- chainnose pliers
- roundnose pliers
- cutters
- ruler

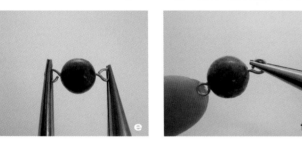

Form the loops

Slide the bead onto the wire **a**. Using roundnose pliers, form a link loop away from you on Mark 2 for 20-gauge wire and Mark 1 for 22-gauge wire. Straighten the loop.

Push the bead to the loop, and trim the wire ⅜ in. (9.5mm) past the bead for 20-gauge and ⁵⁄₁₆ in. (8mm) past the bead for 22-gauge wire **b**. With chainnose pliers, bend the cut wire above the bead toward the open side of the loop **c**. Form a second loop with roundnose pliers **d**.

With two pairs of pliers, adjust the loops so they are symmetrical **e**.

Open and close the loops

Hold the link loop at a slight angle just before the gap in the wire with chainnose pliers. Push the tip of the chainnose pliers away from you to open the loop **f**. Bring the tip back toward you to close the loop.

HEADPIN

Make a headpin easily by hammering the tip of a wire flat enough that the bead can't slip off.

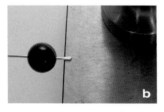

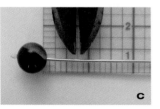

Materials
- 20- or 22-gauge dead-soft or half-hard wire
- bead

Tools
- roundnose pliers
- cutters
- chasing hammer
- bench block
- ruler

Slide a bead onto the wire.

Put the tip of the wire on the edge of the bench block **a**. Hammer the tip three or four times to flatten it **b**. Slide the bead down to check that it won't slide off. Hammer more if needed.

Push the bead to the flattened end. Trim the wire ⅜ in. (9.5mm) above the bead for 20-gauge wire and ⁵⁄₁₆ in. (8mm) for 22-gauge wire **c**. Using roundnose pliers, bend the wire **d** and form a loop away from you on Mark 2 for 20-gauge and Mark 1 for 22-gauge wire **e**.

WRAPPED LOOP

Making a wrapped loop is an important technique to master. It makes a completely closed loop. Many basics and links in the following projects call for wrapped loops.

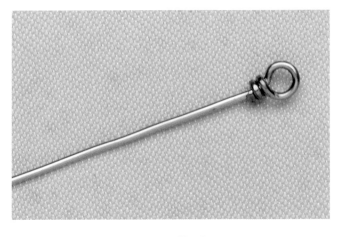

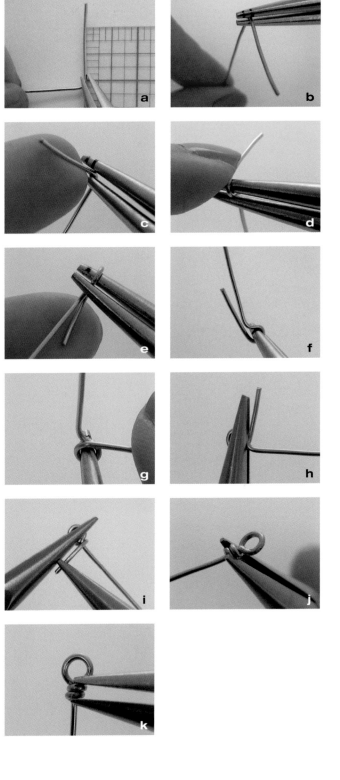

Materials
- 20-, 22-, or 24-gauge dead-soft or half-hard wire

Tools
- roundnose pliers
- 2 pairs of chainnose pliers
- cutters
- ruler

Make a perpendicular bend in the wire ¾ in. (19mm) from the end of 20-gauge wire, and ⅝ in. (16mm) from the end of 22- and 24-gauge wire **a**.

Using Mark 2 for 20-gauge and Mark 1 for 22- and 24-gauge wire, place the roundnose pliers next to the bend in the wire **b**. With your fingers, bring the wire up and around the top jaw of the roundnose pliers until it touches the other end of the wire **c-f**. Readjust the pliers, and continue forming the wire around the pliers to form a complete circle **g**. At this point, you can slip on a finished bead link or pre-made chain link per the projects instructions.

Firmly grasp the circle perpendicularly with chainnose pliers **h**. Wrap the short wire around the straight wire with a second pair of chainnose pliers **i**.

Pinch the end of the wrapping wire with chainnose pliers to tuck it to the wrap **j**. If needed, use chainnose pliers to squeeze the wrapped section together to get rid of any gaps **k**.

WRAPPED LOOP BEAD LINK

A wrapped loop bead link is more complicated and more decorative than a plain bead link. To connect wire wrapped loops to each other or to pre-made chain, the link must be slipped into the wrapped loop while it's being formed.

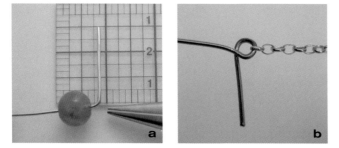

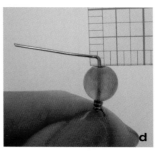

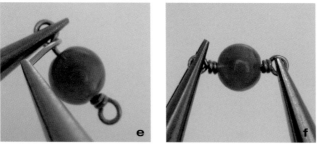

Materials
• 20-, 22-, or 24-gauge dead-soft wire
• bead

Tools
• 2 pairs of chainnose pliers
• roundnose pliers
• cutters
• ruler

Slide a bead onto the wire.

Use chainnose pliers to make a perpendicular bend in the wire ¾ in. (19mm) from the end for 20-gauge wire, and ⅝ in. (16mm) from the end for 22- and 24-gauge wire **a**. Form a wrapped loop on Mark 2 for 20-gauge, and Mark 1 for 22- and 24-gauge wire (adding a chain or a link at the halfway point if called for in the instructions **b**).

Push the bead to the wrapped loop, and with the ruler, cut the wire ⅞ in. (22mm) from the top of the bead for 20-gauge wire, and ¾ in. (19mm) for 22- and 24-gauge wire **c**. Measure up ¹⁄₁₆ in. (1.5mm) from the bead and use chainnose pliers to bend the wire perpendicularly **d**. Form a second wrapped loop **e**.

Adjust the loops to make them symmetrical **f**.

NOTE: 20-gauge wire can be stiff and hard to wrap, but depending on the size of your bead and your project, it may be what you need. Work slowly and carefully, and keep your wraps snug.

WRAPPED LOOP HEADPIN

A wrapped loop headpin is similar to a wrapped loop bead link, but one end of the wire is hammered to prevent the bead from falling off.

Materials
- 20-, 22-, or 24-gauge dead-soft or half-hard wire
- bead

Tools
- 2 pairs of chainnose pliers
- roundnose pliers
- cutters
- ruler
- chasing hammer
- bench block

String a bead onto the spool of wire. Hammer the tip of the wire flat enough so the bead can't slide off **a**.

Push the bead to the hammered end. Cut the wire ¾ in. (19mm) from the end for 20-gauge wire and ⅝ in. (16mm) from the end for 22- and 24-gauge wire **b**. Make a perpendicular bend in the wire ¹⁄₁₆ in. (1.5mm) above the bead with chainnose pliers **c**. Form a wrapped loop **d, e**. Adjust the loop so it's straight **f**.

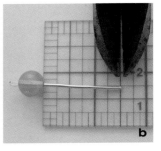

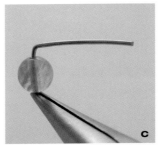

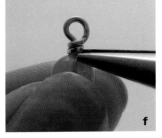

EYE CLASP An eye is one half of the closure of a clasp and is like a non-symmetrical S-link. Because both loops are open, this version is less durable than a wrapped loop eye clasp (p. 28).

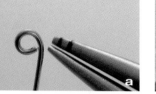

Materials
• 20- or 22-gauge dead-soft or half-hard wire

Tools
• 2 pairs of chainnose pliers
• roundnose pliers
• cutters
• ruler
• chasing hammer
• bench block

Cut a 1-in. (25.5mm) length of 20-gauge wire, or a ¾-in. (19mm) length of 22-gauge wire.

Form a loop on one end of the wire with roundnose pliers, using Mark 2 for 20-gauge wire and Mark 1 for 22-gauge wire **a**.

Firmly hold the loop in a pair of chainnose pliers with the straight wire pointing toward you **b**. Form a larger loop, positioning the wire ¾ of the way down the roundnose pliers, as shown **c, d**.

Hammer the eye on the bench block to work harden it **e**. Hammer the top (larger loop) of the eye a few extra times to help keep the curve **f**.

HOOK CLASP

This quick and easy hook has a link loop that can open and close.

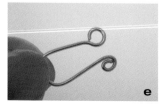

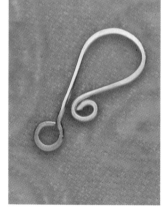

Materials
• 20-gauge (preferable) or 22-gauge dead-soft or half-hard wire

Tools
• chainnose pliers
• roundnose pliers
• cutters
• ruler
• chasing hammer
• bench block

Cut a 1¾-in. (44mm) length of 20-gauge wire, or a 1½-in. (38mm) length of 22-gauge wire.

Using the tip of the roundnose pliers, form almost a full loop on the end of the wire **a**. With chainnose pliers, pinch the loop closed. Hold the loop with chainnose pliers and roll it toward the wire tail over your thumb to make a short spiral **b, c**. Grasp the wire about ¾ in. (19mm) from the loop at the base of the roundnose pliers' jaws. Bend both ends of the wire around one jaw of the pliers, as shown **d**.

On the other end, form a loop with roundnose pliers and straighten the loop **e**. Hold the hook with roundnose pliers and adjust it so the spiral is ⅛ in. (3mm) above the loop **f**. This step also slightly elongates the hook's curve.

On the bench block, hammer the hook to work harden it **g**. Hammer the curve on the hook to flatten it and for extra support **h**.

Sometimes, you'll need to use chainnose pliers to turn the loop perpendicular to the hook **i**. The project instructions will specify if the loop should be turned perpendicular.

With chainnose pliers, bend the loop slightly up **j**. This makes the eye slip more easily into the hook.

Attach the hook to an eye or chain, with the hook facing down and the link loop opening in the back.

TOGGLE CLASP
Adding a jump ring can help the toggle swivel properly.

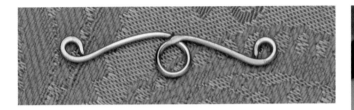

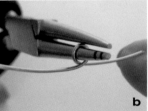

Materials
- 20-gauge dead-soft or half-hard wire

Tools
- chainnose pliers
- roundnose pliers
- cutters
- ruler
- chasing hammer
- bench block

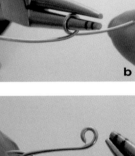

Cut a 2-in. (51mm) length of wire.

Center the wire in the jaws of roundnose pliers, approximately ⅓ of the way down. Bend the wire ends toward each other and in opposite directions **a, b, c**.

Form a loop on each end of the wire, rolling it above and toward the center loop using Mark 2 **d**. Make any adjustments needed so the toggle is symmetrical. Slide the center loop on one jaw of the roundnose pliers, and push down on the end loops to curve the wire **e, f**.

On the bench block, hammer the toggle to work harden it **g**.

Reshape the curve of the bar again as you did earlier **h**. (Close the end loops with chainnose pliers if they spring open during hammering **i**.)

Connect a jump ring to the link loop of the toggle, if called for in the instructions.

Basics

WRAPPED LOOP EYE CLASP

The wrapped loop eye can connect to other links by opening and closing the link loop. The eye is wrapped closed for security.

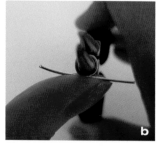

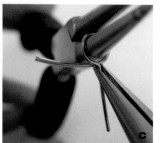
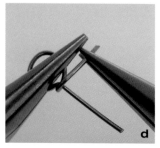

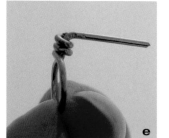

Materials
• 20- or 22-gauge dead-soft or half-hard wire

Tools
• 2 pairs of chainnose pliers
• roundnose pliers
• wire cutters
• ruler
• chasing hammer
• bench block

Cut 1¾-in. (44mm) of 20-gauge wire, or 1½ in. (38mm) of 22-gauge wire.

Center the wire in the jaw of the roundnose pliers at the base **a**. Wrap each end around the base until they cross **b**. Bend one of the wire ends perpendicular to the other **c**.

Hold the eye at the joint with one pair of chainnose pliers. Wrap the other wire around the bent wire with a second pair of chainnose pliers **d**. Reshape the loop with the roundnose pliers, if needed.

With roundnose pliers, form a loop away from you on Mark 2 for 20-gauge and Mark 1 for 22- and 24-gauge wire **e, f**. (Some projects call for the loop to remain parallel. The instructions will let you know.)

Hammer the link on the bench block, avoiding the wrapped section, to work harden.

WRAPPED LOOP HOOK CLASP

This secure wrapped loop hook has a link loop that cannot be opened. It must be connected to a link or to a piece while forming the wrapped loop. The 22-gauge loop is formed on Mark 2 for flexibility and to better accommodate links.

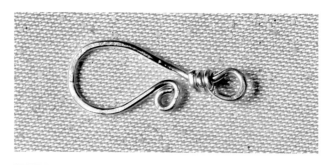

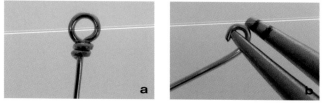

Materials
• 20- or 22-gauge dead-soft or half-hard wire

Tools
• 2 pairs of chainnose pliers
• roundnose pliers
• cutters
• ruler
• chasing hammer
• bench block

Cut a 2¼-in. (2.25cm) length of 20-gauge wire or 2 in. (51mm) of 22-gauge wire.

Measure ¾ in. (19mm). Make a perpendicular bend in the wire with chainnose pliers ¾ in. from the end for 20-gauge wire and ⅝ in. (16mm) from the end for 22-gauge wire. Make a wrapped loop on Mark 2 **a**.

Using the tip of roundnose pliers, form almost a full loop at the very end of the wire **b**. With chainnose pliers, pinch the loop together and continue to curve against the straight wire as shown, **c, d**. Curve the approximate center of the straight wire around the base of the roundnose pliers. With roundnose pliers, pull the hook so it is about ⅛ in. (3mm) above the wrapped section **e**.

Avoiding the wrapped section, hammer the hook and loop on the bench block to work harden **f, g**. Hammer the curve on the hook to flatten for extra support.

Bend the wrapped section up slightly so the eye can slip easily into the hook **h**.

Some projects will call for the hook be turned perpendicular to the wrapped loop. With chainnose pliers, turn the loop so it's perpendicular to the hook.

Both perpendicular and non-perpendicular loops should be bent up slightly with chainnose pliers so the eye or chain link slips easily into the hook.

Attach the hook to a chain or eye with the hook facing down.

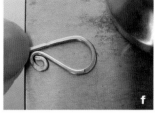

EAR HOOKS

I prefer 22-gauge half-hard wire for ear hooks. You may use craft wire if it doesn't bother your ears, but craft wire isn't as sturdy as silver or gold.

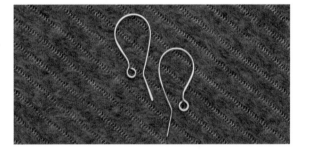

Cut two 2-in. (51mm) pieces of wire. With roundnose pliers, form a loop at one end on both pieces of wire using Mark 1. Straighten the loops.

Hold the wires together so the loops are parallel and bend them over the pen barrel **a** so ¼ in. (6.5mm) of the straight ends extend past the loops **b**. Forming both wires at the same time keeps the ear hooks more symmetrical.

Position chainnose pliers next to the loop and make a slight bend in the wire as shown **c**. Repeat with the other ear hook. Make another slight bend at the other end of the wires adjacent to the bend above the loop **d**. Using your fingers, squeeze the ends of the hook together. Pinch the hook closer together with your fingers **e**.

Working with one ear hook at a time, slightly hammer the curve of the ear hooks to work harden them **f**. Don't hammer too much or they will be uncomfortable to wear. Hammer the rest of the hooks just enough to hold their shape – one or two taps.

Hold both hooks together with one hand so the wire ends are facing up. Working away from you, file the ends of the wire to remove the sharp edges and burrs. I like to feel if there any burrs left with the tips of my fingernails. File until the wire ends are completely smooth.

Some directions specify an ear hook with a perpendicular loop. Use chainnose pliers to gently turn the loop perpendicular to the hook.

Materials
- 22-gauge half-hard or dead-soft wire

Tools
- chainnose pliers
- roundnose pliers
- cutters
- ruler
- pen
- chasing hammer
- bench block
- flat file

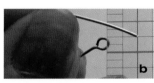

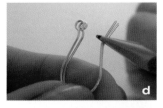

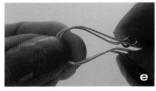

WRAPPED LOOP EAR HOOKS

a

b

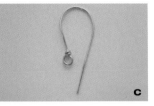

c

d

e

f

g

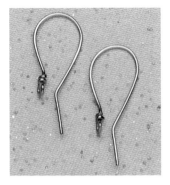

Materials
- 22-gauge half-hard wire

Tools
- 2 pairs of chainnose pliers
- roundnose pliers
- cutters
- ruler
- pen

NOTE: Dead-soft silver, gold, and copper and craft wire are too soft for this design – they don't hold their shape.

Cut two 2¼-in. (2.25cm) pieces of wire. Form a wrapped loop ½ in. (13mm) from the end of each piece of wire. Make two wraps, and tighten the wrapped section with chainnose pliers **a**.

Aligning the loops, hold both wires together and bend them around the pen barrel **b**, leaving straight wire ends ¼ in. (6.5mm) longer than the loops **c**. Turn the loops perpendicular with chainnose pliers, so they face forward **d**. With chainnose pliers, make a slight bend in the wire above the loop as shown **e**. Repeat with the second earring wire.

Continue forming the hooks simultaneously, and use chainnose pliers to make a slight bend in the straight wires **f**. Pinch the bend and the loop close together with your fingers.

Hammer the curve of the hook on a bench block to work harden. Don't hammer the hook too much or it will be uncomfortable in your ear. Hammer the rest of the hook (avoiding the wrapped sections) with one or two taps to work harden.

Hold both hooks firmly with your fingers so the ends are facing up. Filing away from you, file the ends to remove the sharpness and the burrs **g**. Feel the filed ends with your fingertips and nails to see if any burrs were left behind. File until completely smooth.

WRAPPING A BEAD BETWEEN A DOUBLE WIRE

Adding a decorative bead to an open wire link is a nice finishing touch. I'm using a link similar to the Pea pod earrings on p. 84 to demonstrate this technique.

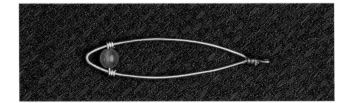

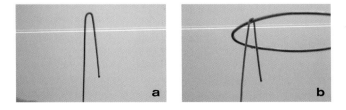

a

b

Materials
- wire link
- bead
- 24-gauge wire

Tools
- chainnose pliers
- cutters
- ruler

Cut a 1½-in. (38mm) length of 24-gauge wire, unless otherwise specified in the project instructions. Form a "U" or hook shape ½ in. (13mm) from an end of the wire with chainnose pliers **a**. Hook the bent wire over the link with the longer wire across the top **b**.

Holding the long wire in place with your thumb and forefinger **c**, wrap the short wire around the link three times (or as directed) with chainnose pliers. Leave the excess. Squeeze the wraps together with chainnose pliers **d**.

String the bead on the long wire **e**. The straight wire should be on top of the link. Wrap the straight wire around the link three times (or as directed). Make sure the second wire wraps are in the same location as the opposite side – above or below the bead. Leave the excess. Squeeze the wraps together with chainnose pliers.

Adjust the location of the wrapped section and bead as directed with your fingers or pliers. On one side, pull the excess wire with chainnose pliers in a curving motion with your hand to tighten. Repeat on the other side, but don't tighten too much or the link will bow. Squeeze the wrapped wire together.

Pull the excess wire behind the link. Cut the excess wire close to the link **f**. Pinch the end of the wire down against the wire link, making sure it doesn't show on the front of the link. Firmly squeeze the wrapped wire with chainnose pliers to flatten, and secure it to the link. Squeeze the wrapped wire together, if it separates, with chainnose pliers **g**.

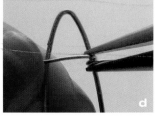

WRAPPING A BEAD ON A SINGLE WIRE

Materials
- wire link
- bead
- 24-gauge wire

Tools
- chainnose pliers
- cutters
- ruler

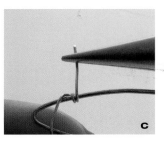

Cut a 1½-in. (38mm) length of wire, unless otherwise directed. Form a "U" or a hook shape ½ in. (13mm) from one end of the wire. Hook the bent wire on the link so the shorter wire is across the top **a**. Pinch the long wire in place with your thumb and forefinger, and wrap the short wire around the link three times (or as directed) with chainnose pliers. Leave the excess. Squeeze the wraps together with chainnose pliers **b**.

With chainnose pliers, make a bend in the long wire above the wraps, about ¹⁄₁₆ in. (1.5mm) from the base as shown (or as directed – usually the height of the bead hole) **c**. String the bead **d**. Bend the wire down behind the link **e**. Wrap the wire around the link three times (or as specified) with chainnose pliers. Squeeze the wraps together **f**.

Adjust the location of the wrapped section and bead. On one side, pull on the excess wire with chainnose pliers to tighten **g**. Repeat on the other side, but don't tighten too much or the link will bow. Squeeze the wraps together.

Cut the excess wire behind the link. With chainnose pliers, pinch down the end of the wrapping wire **h**. Center the bead over the link by squeezing together the wire that goes into the bead hole. Firmly squeeze the wrapped wire with chainnose pliers to flatten and secure it to the link. If it separates, squeeze together the wrapped wire with chainnose pliers.

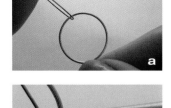

Using the Basics

This chapter takes the basics learned in Chapter 1 and puts them to good use. The projects presented here start simply with the more basic link loops and findings, and then progress to more complicated wrapped loops. Pre-made chain in most of the projects helps you complete them faster. This is the only chapter that uses pre-made anything. The last two projects, however, will take a longer time to complete because you'll make the chain entirely by hand. All of these pieces offer great practice for learning and implementing basic wire jewelry links and techniques.

Wire shaping, hammering, and adding a bead are the techniques used to create these elegant earrings. Half-hard wire is best suited for this piece because its rigidness helps the earrings keep their shape after many uses. You may use craft wire, but the shape may begin to deteriorate over time. Refer to p. 29 for additional guidance on forming the hook.

Materials
- 2 7mm pearls, pale pink
- 22-gauge gold wire, half-hard

Tools
- chainnose pliers
- chasing hammer
- bench block
- pen barrel
- file

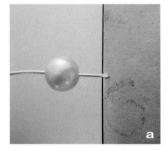

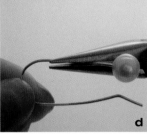

Cut wire into two 2½-in. (64mm) pieces. Slide a pearl onto one of the wires. Move the pearl away from the wire's end (to avoid hitting it with the hammer), and hammer the tip of the wire on a bench block **a**. Slide the pearl down to the flattened end.

Form a hook by bending the wire in half around a pen barrel **b**. Using chainnose pliers, make a slight bend in the wire ¼ in. (6.5mm) from the un-hammered end **c**. Straighten the wire above the pearl with chainnose pliers, if needed **d**. Pinch the ends of the hook closer together with your fingers.

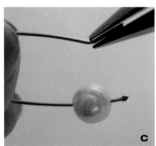

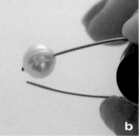

Hammer the hook to work harden it **e**. Tap the curve one or two more times to help keep its shape. To finish, file the ear hook ends smooth and remove all burrs **f**.

Repeat to make a second earring.

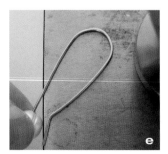

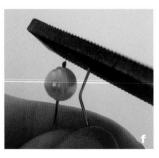

These earrings are short chains comprised of bead links and a headpin. The wrapped loops of the ear hooks add a finished look at the tops and extra texture to the piece. Amorphous pebble beads add more visual interest to an otherwise basic chain. Match the sizes and shapes when selecting the beads for each earring for a more pulled-together look.

Materials
- 4 9–11mm pebble beads, pale pink ice flake quartz
- 4 5–6mm pebble beads, rose quartz
- 22-gauge gold wire, dead soft

Tools
- 2 pairs of chainnose pliers
- roundnose pliers
- cutters
- ruler

Make ahead
- 22-gauge gold wrapped non-perpendicular loop ear hooks (p. 30)

- 4 bead links **a** with 9–11mm beads (p. 22)

- 2 bead links **b** with two 5–6mm beads (p. 22)

- 2 headpins **c** with 5–6mm beads (p. 22)

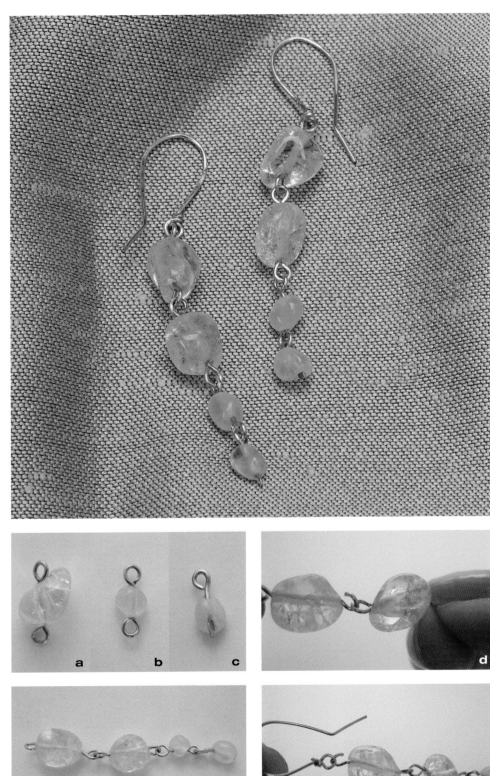

Assemble the earrings **d, e,** by connecting two separate chains in the following order: large bead link, large bead link, small bead link, small headpin.

Finish by connecting an ear hook to the end loop on the chain **f**. Repeat with the other chain and ear hook.

Twisted wire makes its debut in a decorative and functional toggle clasp. If the wire untwists while you're working with it, simply tighten the ends with chainnose pliers. You'll need a steady hand on the final step when the jump ring connects the pendant chain, the last pearl headpin, and the eye. My best advice is to grasp the jump ring firmly and proceed slowly.

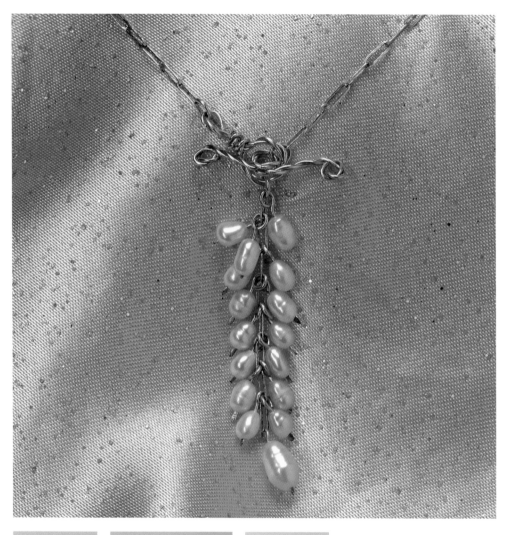

Materials
- 15 3x4mm top-drilled rice pearls, white
- 6x9mm teardrop-shaped top-drilled pearl, white
- 15¾ in. (40cm) chain, sterling silver
- 22-gauge silver wire, half hard

Tools:
- 2 pairs of chainnose pliers
- roundnose pliers
- cutters
- ruler
- chasing hammer
- bench block
- vise

Make ahead
- 8½ in. (21.6cm) twisted silver wire made from 20 in. (50.8cm) of 22-gauge wire (p. 19)
- 3 jump rings using Mark 2 on roundnose pliers (p. 20)
- toggle and wrapped-loop eye (use 2 in. of twisted wire and the 20-gauge wire guide for each) (p. 27, 28)
- 6x9mm pearl headpin (p. 22)
- 15 rice pearl headpins (p. 22)

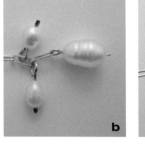

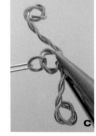

Cut a 14¼-in. (36.2cm) length and a 1½-in. (38mm) length of chain. Attach the large pearl headpin to the bottom link of the 1½-in. chain **a** with a jump ring.

Attach two small pearl headpins to each remaining link on the chain **b**.

Connect the toggle to one end of the 14¼-in. chain with a jump ring **c**.

Connect the small loop of the eye to the other end of the 14¼-in. length of chain with a jump ring **d**.

Connect the last pearl headpin and the short chain with pearls to the large loop of the eye with a jump ring **e**.

These wrapped-loop ear hooks are a touch larger than the hooks in Basics, so the beaded headpins dangle at a more comfortable and flattering space when worn. The wrapped loops are also larger to accommodate the multitude of headpins. Change the feel of these earrings by using different beads and metal. More beads make a greater impact.

Materials:
- 14 7mm pearls, pale pink
- 2 2½-in. (64mm) pieces of half-hard silver wire
- 22-gauge half-hard silver wire

Tools:
- 2 pairs of chainnose pliers
- roundnose pliers
- ruler
- chasing hammer
- bench block

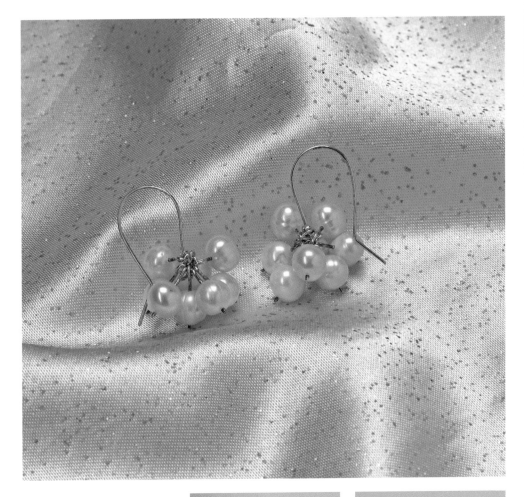

Make two wrapped loop ear hooks **a** with the 2½-in. lengths of wire. Bend the wire ⅝ in. (16mm) from the end and form non-perpendicular loops on Mark 2 (p. 30).

Make 14 pearl headpins (p. 22) with the following changes: Bend the wire ¹⁄₁₆-in. (1.5mm) above the bead **b** and cut the wire ¼-in. (6.5mm) above the bend **c**.

Attach seven headpins to each ear hook's loop **d**.

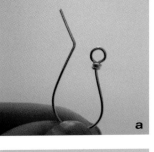

a

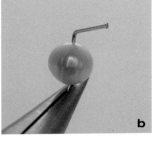

b

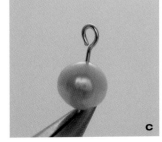

c

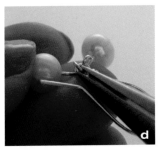

d

Button Pearl Necklace

This necklace is terrific for learning and practicing the wrapped-loop bead link. Basic link loops are used to connect the chains and the bead links. Once you master wrapped loops, the rest of the projects will be much easier.

Materials
- 35 6mm button pearls
- 24-gauge half-hard silver wire
- chain, silver

Tools
- 2 pairs of chainnose pliers
- roundnose pliers
- cutters
- ruler
- chasing hammer
- bench block

Make ahead
- 22-gauge silver hook with perpendicular loop (p. 26)
- 22-gauge silver wrapped eye with non-perpendicular loops (p. 28)

Make eight pearl bead links **a,** forming the loops with ¼ in. (6.5mm) of wire on Mark 1 on your roundnose pliers (p. 22).

Make nine pearl double-wrapped loop links **b**, forming the wrapped loops ⅝ in. (16mm) from the end of the wire on Mark 1 on your roundnose pliers (p. 24).

Make 18 pearl single-wrapped loop bead links **c**, forming the wrapped loops ⅝ in. and the link loop ¼ in. from the end of the wire on Mark 1 on your roundnose pliers.

Make 15 S-links **d**, forming the loops ¼ in. from the end of the wire on Mark 1 on your roundnose pliers (p. 21).

Hammer all the links **e** to work harden and flatten, avoiding the beads and the wrapped sections.

Cut 15 1-in. (25.5mm) lengths of chain.

Connect the links and chains as follows **f, g**: chain, S-link, single wrapped loop link, double wrapped loop link, single wrapped loop, S-link, chain, bead link, chain. Repeat until the chain is 15⅜-in. (39cm) long. Make a second chain with the same pattern 17¾ in. (45.1cm) long.

Open the loop on the hook and attach the end link of the long chain (first) and the end link of the short chain **h**. Close the loop. Repeat for the eye **i**.

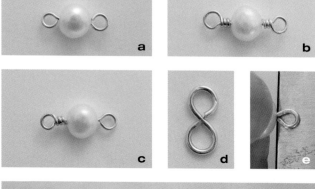

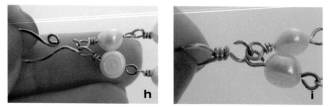

This long necklace is connected with wrapped loop bead links. The pattern is straightforward. The challenge is forming the wrapped loops while connecting the chains. Take your time forming the loops and don't forget to add the chain!

Materials
- 3 3–3.5mm nugget pearls
- 6 4mm round beads, rutilated quartz
- 2 6x9mm teardrop pearls
- 24-gauge silver wire, dead soft
- 36 in. rolo chain, silver with 1.5mm links

Tools
- 2 pairs of chainnose pliers
- roundnose pliers
- wire cutters
- ruler

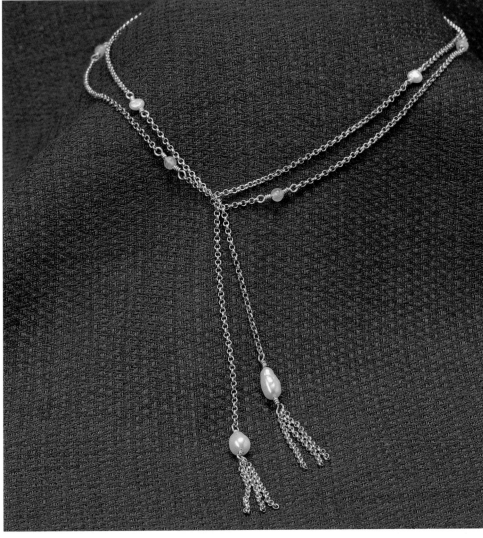

Cut ten 3-in. lengths and six 1-in lengths of chain.

Make a 6x9mm pearl wrapped loop bead link (p. 24) and connect three 1-in. (25.5mm) chains before completing the wrap on the first loop **a, b**. Connect a 3-in. (76mm) chain to the second loop **c**. Finish the wraps **d**.

Connect the remaining chain segments with wrapped loop bead links **e** in the following order: pearl nugget, chain, quartz, chain, quartz, chain, pearl nugget, chain, quartz, chain, quartz, chain, pearl nugget, chain, quartz, chain, quartz, chain. Finish as above, connecting a 6x9mm pearl link to the last segment and then adding three 1-in. lengths of chain to the loop on the other end.

a

b

c

d

e

This three-layered necklace calls for two types of chain. The center chain is connected by wrapped loop bead links. The top and bottom chains are decorated with wire-wrapped link-loop teardrop beads. Be sure to measure the chain accurately for a symmetrical necklace. Another way to keep the chain lengths precise is to count the links. Take note of the instructions for the teardrop bead links; this type of wire-wrapped link loop is used in many projects in later chapters.

Materials
- 12 5x7mm top-drilled briolettes, garnet
- 12 6mm disc-shaped beads, garnet
- 24-gauge gold wire, dead soft
- 2x4mm oval link gold-filled chain

Tools
- 2 pairs of chainnose pliers
- roundnose pliers
- cutters
- ruler
- chasing hammer
- bench block

Make ahead
- 22-gauge gold perpendicular-loop wrapped loop hook (p. 28)
- 22-gauge gold perpendicular-loop wrapped loop eye clasp (p. 28)

Cut a 15-in. (38.1cm) and a 19-in. (48.3cm) length of chain.

Cut 12 1½-in. (38mm) pieces of wire. Slide a briolette onto a wire and cross the wire ends evenly above the bead's point, leaving a small gap **a**. At the cross, bend the front wire perpendicular to the back wire **b, c**. With chainnose pliers, hold the crossed wires just below the joint. Using a second pair of pliers and your other hand, wrap the perpendicular wire three times around the straight wire **d**. Pinch the wraps together, if needed, and trim the excess wire to ¼ in. (6.5mm) **e**. Form a bead loop away from you with roundnose pliers on Mark 1 **f**. Hammer the loops on the bench block to work harden. Repeat with the remaining briolettes to make 12 drop links.

Short chain:

Use chainnose pliers to attach a garnet drop link to the center link of the 15-in. chain **g**. Attach a garnet drop bead link 1¼ in. (32mm) from each side of the center link **h**.

Long chain:

Attach a garnet drop link to the center link of the 19-in. chain **g**. Attach three more drop bead links 1¼ in. from each side of the center link **h**.

Center chain:

Cut 11 ¾-in. (19mm) and 2 1¾-in. (44mm) lengths of chain. Connect a 1¾-in. chain to a wrapped loop disc bead (p. 24). Add a ¾-in. chain to the second wrapped loop. Repeat, alternating disc wrapped bead links and ¾-in. chains **i, j**. The second wrapped loop on the last connects to the remaining 1¾-in. chain. The finished chain is 17½ in. (43.2mm) long.

Finishing the necklace

Squeeze the eye in the chainnose pliers to form an oval **k**. Pinch and adjust the oval shape with chainnose pliers **l**. Hammer to work harden, avoiding the wraps.

Open the loop end on the hook with the hook facing up. Connect the chains in the following order: short, center, and long **m**. Close the loop. Don't twist or tangle the chain. Open the loop on the eye, and connect the other ends of the chain in the same order. Close the loop.

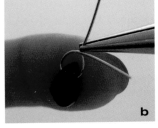

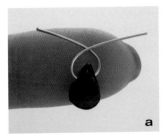

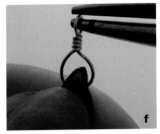

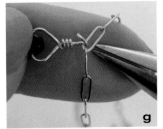

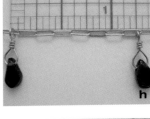

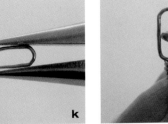

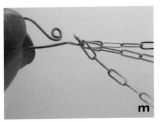

Movement, color, and noise make this bracelet one of my favorite pieces. Half-drilled beads decorate the handmade S-link chain. The card stock and tape display tip is a handy way to avoid getting glue all over your fingers. I highly recommend making one.

Materials
- 19 6mm half-drilled beads, amethyst
- 19 6mm half-drilled beads, white pearl
- 12 8mm half-drilled beads, rose quartz
- 20-gauge silver wire, half-hard

Tools
- chainnose pliers
- roundnose pliers
- wire cutters
- ruler
- card stock and low-tack tape display (see step 2)
- Loctite 454 glue
- mask
- paper

Make ahead
- 25 20-gauge half-hard silver S-links (p. 21)
- 20-gauge half-hard silver wrapped loop hook with perpendicular loop (p. 28)
- 20-gauge half-hard silver wrapped loop eye with perpendicular loop (p. 28)

Make the bead links

Form a bead-link loop with 20-gauge wire on Mark 2 of your round-nose pliers **a**. Trim the wire ¼ in. (6.5mm) past the loop for 8mm beads and ⅛ in. (3mm) for 6mm beads. Slip a bead on the wire to check the length, and trim the wire shorter if needed. (Some bead holes are deeper than others.) Leave a small space between the loop and the bead, so you don't damage the bead when opening and closing a loop and for easier gluing **b**. Remove the bead from the wire loop. Make 50 loops.

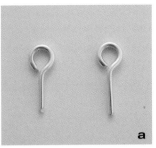

Card stock and low tack tape display

This handy tool holds the beads in place as you glue the bead and the wire loop together. Cut a sheet of card stock 1½-in. (38mm) wide and punch holes every ½ in. (13mm) on both sides of the sheet with a hole punch. Put low-tack tape on the back of the card stock. Many bulk-sold half-drilled pairs of pearls come on a similar display. If your pearls come this way, use the display instead of making one.

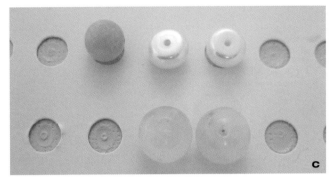

Glue the beads

Place the beads on the tape display with the holes facing up **c**. Working on three to four beads at time **d**, slowly fill the hole with glue and insert the wire loop's stem into the hole, making sure the loop doesn't touch the glue (it might get glued shut). The glue dries very quickly. After about a minute, remove the beads from the tape by grasping the bead and not the wire. Let them dry completely on the piece of paper on the table for a few hours or overnight. Repeat for a total of 50 glued bead units.

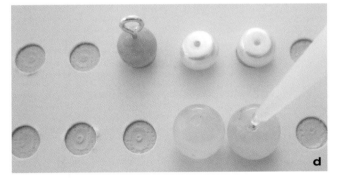

Assemble the chain

Link the S-links together to form a chain **e**. Attach one bead unit to each loop of the S-link chain **f**.

Finish the bracelet

Attach the hook to the end loop on one end of the S-link chain, and attach the eye to the other end loop. Test the link connections by holding the bracelet a few inches above your work table and dropping it a few times to see if any beads fall off. If they do, take off the link and reattach the beads following the above steps.

This necklace takes a while to complete because it's made entirely by hand. When making so many S-links, break the process into steps: Form the first loop and cut it to size. Then after making a large pile of half-formed links, finish the second loops. It seems to go faster that way. Although everything else is handmade, I prefer a store-bought headpin, because the head of the pin sits flush against the bead.

Materials
- 20-gauge gold wire, dead-soft
- 11 6mm beads, glass pearls
- 12mm bead, glass pearl
- 20-gauge gold headpin (store bought)

Tools
- 2 pairs of chainnose pliers
- roundnose pliers
- wire cutters
- ruler

Make ahead
- 20-gauge gold wrapped loop hook with a perpendicular loop (p. 28)
- 20-gauge gold wrapped loop eye with non-perpendicular loop (p. 28)
- 59 S-links (p. 21)
- 11 6mm pearl bead links (p. 22)

Assemble the necklace

Make a headpin with the 12mm pearl and the store-bought headpin **a**: Slide a 12mm pearl on a head pin and trim the wire to ⅜ in. (9.5mm) above the bead. Make a loop using Mark 2 on your roundnose pliers.

Make two 8-in. (20.3cm) chains: Alternate five S-links and a bead link **b, c**. Open the loop on a remaining bead link and connect it to the S-link ends of both chains **d**. Attach a chain of five S-links to the other loop on the bead link **e**. Attach the large pearl headpin to the end S-link of the short chain **f**.

Finish the necklace

Connect the eye to an end bead link with two S-links **g**. Connect the hook to the other end bead link with two S-links **h**.

a

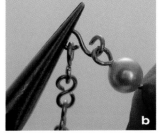

b

c

d

e

f

g

h

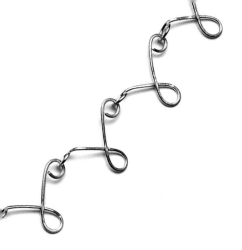

Using a Jig

A jig is a useful tool that makes link shaping easier and more uniform. Jigs range in type and style from a block of wood with nails used as pegs to machine-made plates. The jig used in this book is a small peg board with pegs in various sizes. The holes are in a grid pattern, so all of the creativity is up to you. Lay the pegs out in a pattern, and wrap the wire around the pegs in a specific manner. The process photos are essential for following the wrapping in the projects. The first project, *How to use a jig*, is full of tips and techniques. Keep referring to it when working on projects in this chapter. Knowing the basics and how to use them will help you complete these pieces. Every project in this chapter uses some sort of basic piece or technique. After learning these techniques, you'll be able to manipulate plain wire into sculptural links.

A jig is useful for shaping and keeping links symmetrical because the wire is wrapped around pegs laid out in a pattern. Since the wire is so flimsy after shaping, I prefer to hammer the pieces to work harden them on most projects. Keep referring back to these instructions when trying the other projects in this chapter; they include many helpful tips and techniques for using a jig. For photo clarity, I painted the jig white and put a piece of paper behind the pegs in the wrapping process photos. Also for clarity, the pegs are color coded according to size.

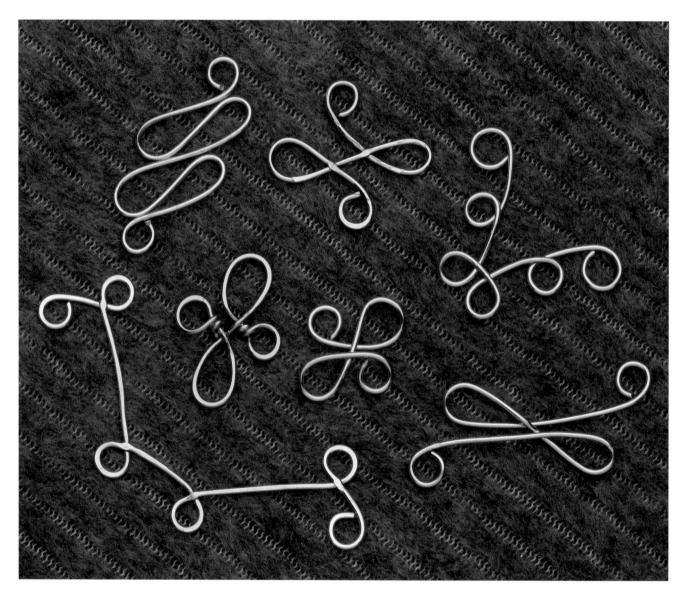

Materials
- 20- or 22-gauge dead-soft wire or craft wire
- beads (optional)

Tools
- Thing-A-Ma-Jig Deluxe
- pegs of various sizes (all included with the jig)
- chainnose pliers
- roundnose pliers
- cutters
- ruler
- chasing hammer
- bench block

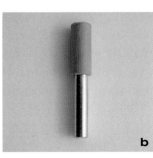
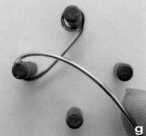

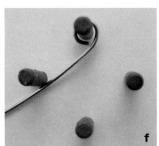
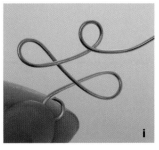
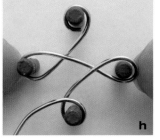

Position the design on the jig

The peg sizes are color coded for clarity: small=blue **a**, medium=yellow **b**, large=green **c**. Position four small pegs in the holes as pictured **d**.

Mark the roundnose pliers

Mark your roundnose pliers ½ in. (13mm) down from the tip. This is the mark to make a jig loop. Form the beginning loop on the new mark to fit around the small blue peg. Don't straighten the loop **e**.

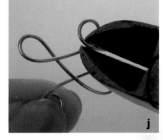

Form the link on the jig

(To make it easier to see, I put a piece of paper behind the pegs.) Slip the loop onto the first peg **f**. Wrap the wire, using chainnose pliers and your fingers, around the pegs as shown **g**. Keep the wire taut, but not too tight, or the wire will pull the pegs out. Try to keep all the loops symmetrical. To prevent the wire from slipping off the pegs as you form the links, push the wire down to the base of the pegs with chainnose pliers. After you form the last loop around the last peg, leave the excess wire and gently remove the link from the jig **h** by putting your nails or fingertips under the link and pulling up. Don't yank the wire in one spot or pull too hard, because the link can become easily misshapen.

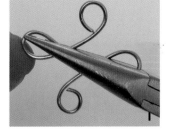

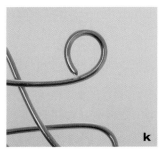

Adjust the link

Trim the excess wire at a slight angle **i, j, k** and use chainnose pliers to flatten the link slightly **l**. Make any adjustments to the link with your fingers, roundnose pliers **m**, and chainnose pliers to make the link symmetrical **n**.

Hammer the link

Hammer the link two to three times on each side (or as directed) to work harden. Only hammer the joints two or three times per side. Hammering will make the joints fuse together – thus making the link sturdy – but too much hammering will make them brittle. If you'd like, flatten the link after the initial hammering to work harden focus on the loops and edges around the joint **o**.

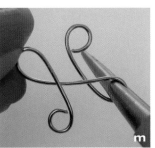

TIP: For some projects, you will need to form the link in the opposite direction (by flipping the link over while wrapping around pegs), so be sure to read through the instructions before beginning.

A simple pattern and swirling design make this an excellent jumping-off point for using a jig. The multiple links and a basic shape are good practice for keeping the links symmetrical while shaping. The small amount of manipulation after shaping gives a taste of what it's like to work with more complicated links. Remember – don't hammer the joints too much, or the wire will break.

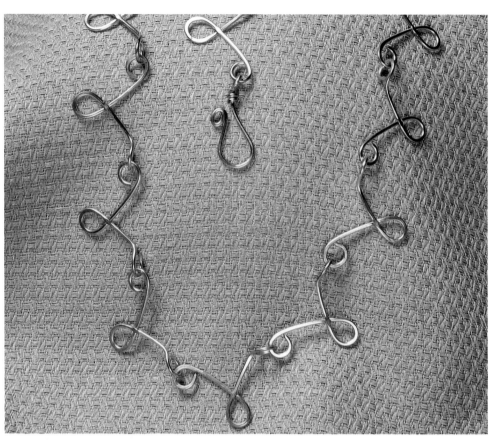

Materials
• 20-gauge gold wire, dead-soft

Tools
• jig
• 3 small pegs
• chainnose pliers
• roundnose pliers
• cutters
• ruler
• chasing hammer
• bench block

Make ahead
• 20-gauge gold wrapped loop hook with perpendicular loop (p. 28)
• 20-gauge gold wrapped loop eye with non-perpendicular loop (p. 28)

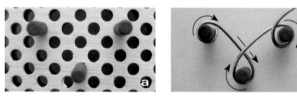

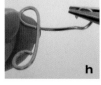

Shape and hammer the links
Cut 22 3½-in. (89mm) long pieces of wire. Form a jig loop at the end of a piece of wire with roundnose pliers. Position the pegs on the jig as shown **a**. Slip the loop onto the top left peg and form the link, working to the right **b**. Remove the link, make any adjustments needed **c**, and trim the excess wire at an angle **d**. Make all adjustments with pliers or your fingers so the link is symmetrical. Repeat with the remaining 3½-in. wires.

Hammer each link two or three times to flatten it.

Using roundnose pliers, straighten the loop's right link **e**, turn the loop so the opening faces the back of the link **f**, and bend the loop down so it's perpendicular to the other loop **g**. Repeat with all the links.

Assemble the necklace
Open the perpendicular loop on a link with chainnose pliers **h** and connect it to the left loop on a second link **i**. Close the loop. Repeat, connecting all the links.

Finish the necklace
Attach the hook to the regular loop on the left end of the chain **j** and the eye to the perpendicular loop at the other end of the chain.

The pattern for these earrings is detailed, so keep an eye out when looping the wire around the pegs. Try to make all the loops the same size. The initial loop is a wrapped loop made on the jig-loop mark of your roundnose pliers. This finished loop adds some weight to these airy earrings.

Materials
- 20-gauge silver wire, half-hard
- 22-gauge silver wire, half-hard
- 12 4mm round beads, rutilated quartz

Tools
- jig
- 7 small pegs
- chainnose pliers
- roundnose pliers
- cutters
- ruler
- chasing hammer
- bench block

Make ahead
- 2 silver ear hooks with non-perpendicular loops (p. 29)
- 12 22-gauge quartz-bead head pins (p. 22)

Form and hammer the links

Cut two 6-in. (15.2cm) pieces of 20-gauge wire. Make a bend in each wire ⅞ in. (22mm) from the end and form a wrapped loop **a** on the jig mark on your roundnose pliers (p. 23).

Position seven pegs as shown **b**. Form a link following the pattern. Place a wrapped loop on the first (left) peg, and wrap the length of the wire as shown, with one length of wire **c**. Make adjustments to the link with pliers and your fingers so the link is symmetrical **d** and the wrapped loop is straight. Trim the excess wire at an angle **e**. Repeat with the second 6-in. wire to make the second earring.

Gently hammer the links to work harden, avoiding the wrapped section.

Assemble the earrings

Use chainnose pliers to turn the wrapped loop so it is perpendicular to the link **f**. Connect a beaded headpin to each loop **g**.

Attach an ear hook to each wrapped loop **h**.

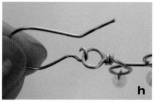

You'll practice many techniques as you make this flowing bracelet. After shaping on the jig, the links need a fair amount of manipulation to get their rounded symmetrical shape. Take your time to make the links identical, and ensure you have proper form when hammering. If the head of the hammer is tilted on the initial blows, the link will get misshapen. Both the hook and the eye are beaded to keep the circular flow of the bracelet.

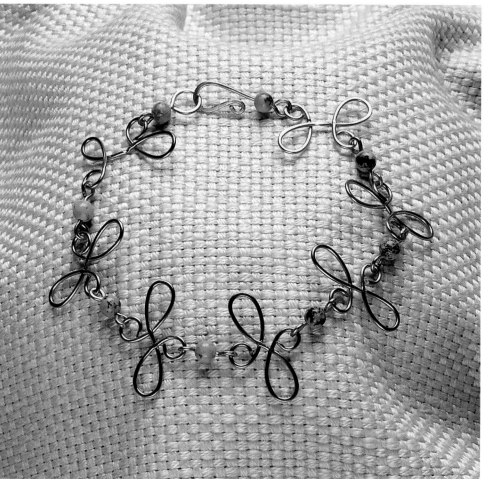

Materials
- 8 4mm round beads, African turquoise
- 20-gauge copper wire

Tools
- jig
- 4 small pegs
- 2 medium pegs
- chainnose pliers
- roundnose pliers
- cutters
- ruler
- chasing hammer
- bench block

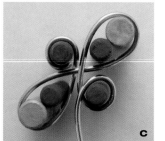

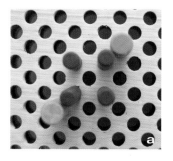

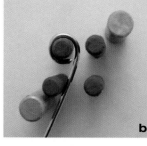

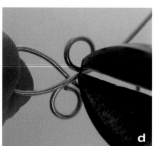

Make the links

Position the pegs on the jig following the pattern **a**. Cut seven 3½-in. (89mm) pieces of 20-gauge wire. Using roundnose pliers, make a jig loop at one end of a wire. Follow the pattern on the jig with the cut wire **b, c**. Adjust the loops so they are symmetrical and trim the excess wire at an angle **d**. Repeat with the remaining 3½-in. wires.

Hammer the links two or three times on the bench block to flatten. Repeat with the remaining links.

Make six turquoise bead links (p. 22) and flatten the loops.

Assemble the bracelet

Open a loop on a bead link and connect it to a small loop on a jig link **e**. Connect a bead link to the second small loop of the jig link. Continue connecting the jig links with bead links for a chain.

Make a beaded hook and eye

Make a hook (p. 26) with the following changes: slide a bead on the wire before forming the loop **f**. Make the link loop, and adjust the hook end so it is slightly above the bead **g**. Don't turn the loop

perpendicular. Hammer to flatten, avoiding the bead.
Make an eye (p. 26), with the following changes: Slide a bead onto the spool of wire and form a loop on Mark 2 of your roundnose pliers. Position the bead next to the loop, and trim the wire ⅝ in. (16mm) from the bead **h**. Form the eye with roundnose pliers. Use chainnose pliers to turn the link loop perpendicular **i**. Hammer the eye to flatten, avoiding the bead.

Finish the bracelet

Connect the hook to the small loop at one end of the bracelet **j**, and connect the eye to the small loop at the other end of the bracelet **k**.

Make an extra set of jig links, two beaded headpins, and a pair of earring wires, and you'll have this darling pair of matching earrings.

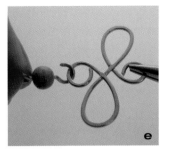

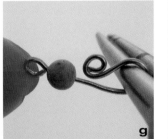

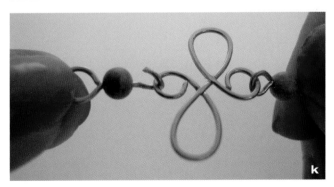

This necklace has two link patterns. The layouts of the patterns are more complicated than what we've done so far. Also, we'll add a bead to the larger link during the shaping on the jig. Take care to avoid the bead when hammering. A few hammer taps will harden the links enough to keep their shape. This is still a delicate piece, so take care not to tug or stretch the links because they will warp.

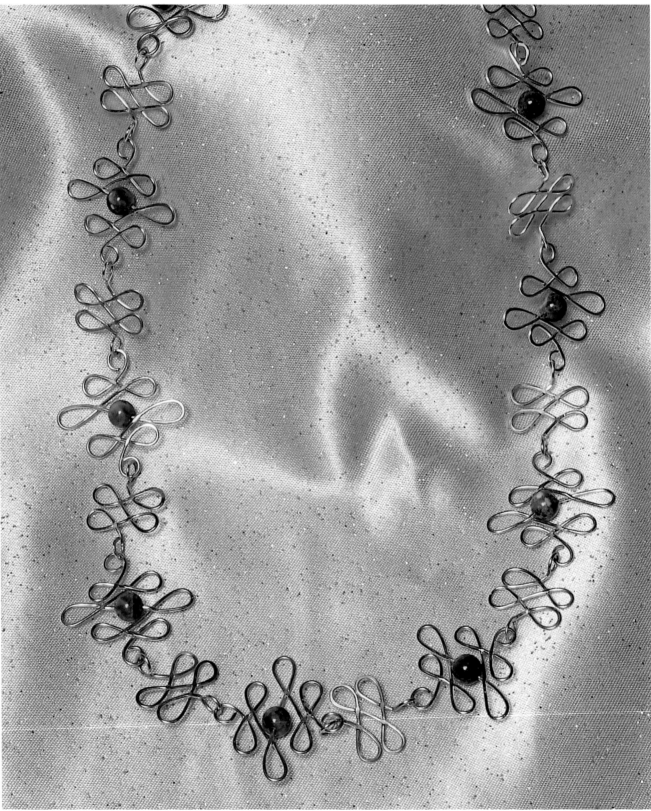

Materials
- 20-gauge silver wire
- 10 6mm round beads, sodalite

Tools
- jig
- 8 small pegs
- chainnose pliers
- roundnose pliers
- cutters
- ruler
- chasing hammer
- bench block

Make ahead
- 20-gauge silver hook with non-perpendicular loop (p. 26)

Make the large bead links
Cut 10 8-in. (20.3cm) pieces of wire.

Position the pegs on the jig as shown **a**. Make a jig loop on the end of an 8-in. wire. Place the loop on the top center peg and form the first half of the link, following the pattern **b**. Slide a bead on the wire in the middle of the pattern **c**. Form the second half of the link with chainnose pliers and use your fingers to adjust the loops as needed to make the links symmetrical **d**. Remove the link from the jig, and trim the excess wire **e**. Hammer the link to work harden the wire, avoiding the bead. Repeat to make a total of 10 bead links.

Make the small links
Cut 11 6-in. (15.2cm) pieces of wire.

Position the pegs on the jig as shown **f**. Make a jig loop at the end of a 6-in. piece of wire. Place the loop on the top center peg and form the link following the pattern **g**. Remove the link from the jig, and trim the excess wire. Use chainnose pliers and your fingers to adjust the loops as needed to make the link symmetrical. Hammer the link two to three times to work harden **h**. Turn the end loops so they are perpendicular to the large middle loop, so the open part of the link loop is facing back **i**. Repeat to make a total of 11 small links.

Assemble the necklace
Connect the links, alternating small and large links **j**, by opening the loops on the small links so the large links keep their shape. Attach the hook to the end loop on one side of the chain **k** and use the end loop on the other side of the necklace as the eye **l**.

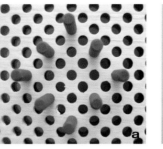

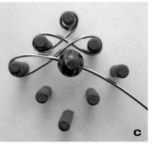

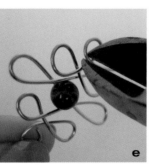

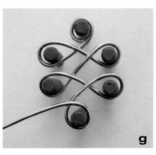

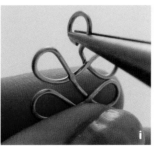

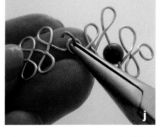

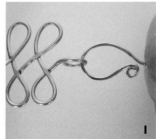

Large, ornate earrings can be a focal accessory for any outfit. This is the most complicated jig pattern in the book. Many pegs are used, but the center pegs only are used as guides. Look closely at the pictures to see where to loop the wire. The tiny wire-wrapped amethyst beads serve a couple of purposes: They are used for decoration, as well as to secure the tops and bottoms of the earrings. Without the wrapping, the earrings would be flimsy and would not hold their shape.

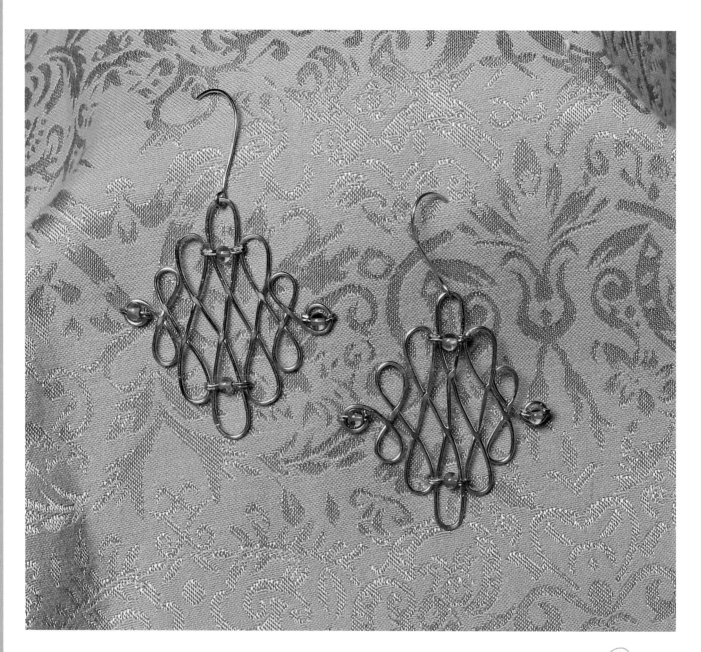

Materials
- 30 in. (76.2cm) 20-gauge gold wire, dead-soft
- 24-gauge gold wire, dead-soft
- 8 3mm round beads, amethyst

Tools
- jig
- 16 small pegs
- chainnose pliers
- roundnose pliers
- cutters
- ruler
- chasing hammer
- bench block

Make ahead
- gold ear hooks with perpendicular loops (p. 29)

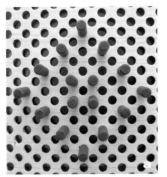

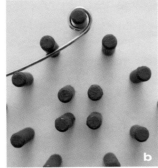

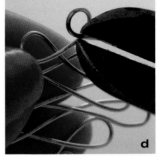

Form and hammer the medallions

Cut two 15-in. (38.1cm) pieces of 20-gauge wire.

Position the pegs on the jig as shown **a**. Using roundnose pliers, make a jig loop large enough to fit a small peg. Place the loop on the top center peg **b** and form the link, working back and forth across the jigs **c**. Trim the excess wire and adjust the medallion shape as needed, so the loops don't overlap **d, e**. Repeat with the second 15-in. wire.

Hammer the links two or three times to flatten **f**.

Wrap the beads

You'll place an amethyst bead in each of the four corners of the medallion. Refer to wrapping a bead between two wires (p. 30), with the following changes: Cut four 1¼-in. (32mm) pieces of 24-gauge wire and make a U-shaped bend ⅜ in. (9.5mm) from the end of each wire **g**. Place the hook on the second side loop on one side of the link. Wrap the short end of the 24-gauge wire around the bottom wire of the second loop and the top wire of the third loop two times **h**. Trim the wrapping wire and slide a bead on the wire and against the wraps, centered in the third loop. Wrap the other end of the 24-gauge wire around the bottom wire of the third loop and the top wire of the fourth loop **i**. Make any adjustments as needed and trim the wire. Repeat on the opposite side of the link.

Wire wrap a bead in the top and bottom center loops as you did before **j, k**.

Repeat to wrap beads to the second medallion.

Complete the earrings

Turn the bead wrapped link and connect an ear hook to the large center loop **l**. Repeat with the second earring.

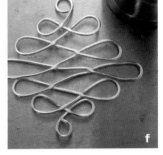

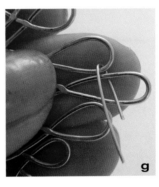

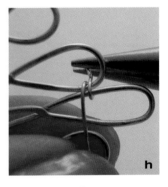

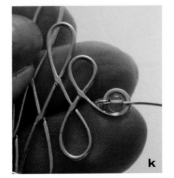

We've now progressed to more sculptural links. You'll practice 11 jig links while making this necklace. You won't need to hammer, because the large amount of manipulation is enough to harden the wire. Keep the links as clean and symmetrical as possible for the best look. By the time you complete this piece, you'll be ready for the next project.

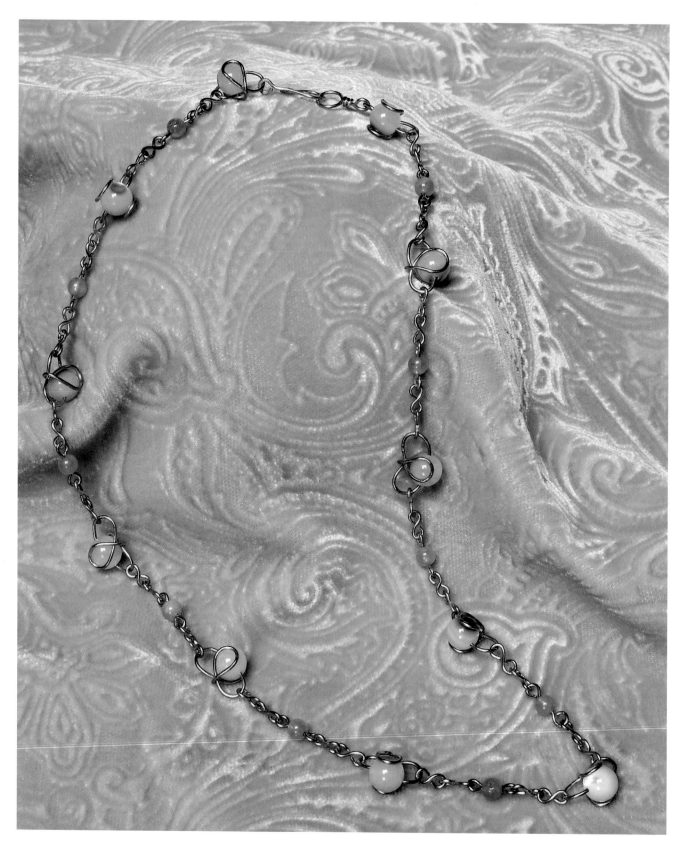

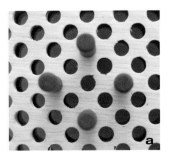
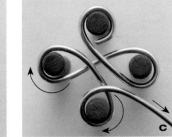
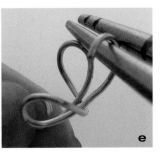
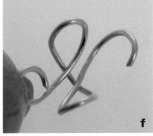
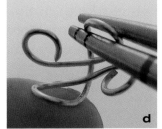
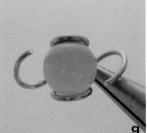
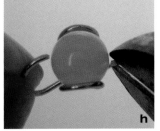
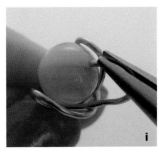

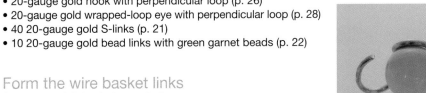

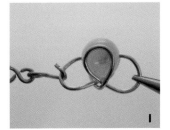
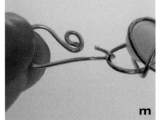

Materials
- 20-gauge gold wire, dead-soft
- 11 8mm round beads, quartz
- 10 5mm beads, green garnet

Tools
- jig
- 4 small pegs
- chainnose pliers
- roundnose pliers
- cutters
- ruler

Make ahead
- 20-gauge gold hook with perpendicular loop (p. 26)
- 20-gauge gold wrapped-loop eye with perpendicular loop (p. 28)
- 40 20-gauge gold S-links (p. 21)
- 10 20-gauge gold bead links with green garnet beads (p. 22)

Form the wire basket links
Cut 11 4-in. (10.2cm) pieces of wire.

Position the pegs on the jig as shown **a**. Make a jig loop at one end of a wire and place it on the top peg. Wrap the wire around the next peg **b**, then **flip the link** and re-position it on the jig. Form the rest of the link, following the pattern **c**.

Trim the excess wire and adjust the link as needed so it is symmetrical. Repeat to make a total of 11 links.

Add the beads
Using roundnose pliers, bend the larger loops inward to slightly curve the center of the link. Repeat with the closed loops to form a basket shape for a quartz bead **d**. Use roundnose pliers to roll open the linking loops **e**, **f**. Put a bead in the "basket" **g**, and pinch the large loops around the bead with your fingers for a tight fit. Cut ¹⁄₁₆ in. (1.5mm) off the end of each open loop **h**. Using chainnose pliers, tuck the wire ends into the bead holes **i**. Gently adjust the wire so it is symmetrical **j**. Repeat with the remaining links and quartz beads.

Complete the necklace
Connect two S-links, a bead link, and two S-links **k**. Connect the chain just made to a wire basket link **l**. Repeat to connect all the basket links.

Connect the hook to the basket link on one end of the necklace **m**. Connect the eye to the other end.

This sweet bracelet is quite a challenge. It requires a lot of link manipulation and reshaping to fit the bead. When forming the link on the jig, don't pull the wire tight; keep it rounded for a softer heart shape. When connecting links with the bead links, make sure the hearts all face the same direction.

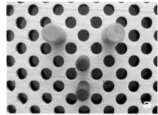

Materials
- 20-gauge gold wire, dead-soft
- 24-gauge gold wire, dead-soft
- 5 6mm round beads, strawberry quartz
- 5 5mm round beads, green garnet

Tools
- jig
- 2 small pegs
- 2 medium pegs
- chainnose pliers
- roundnose pliers
- cutters
- ruler

Make the caged heart links
Cut five 5-in. (12.7cm) lengths of 20-gauge wire.

Position the pegs on the jig as shown **a**. Use roundnose pliers to make a jig loop at one end of a wire, and place it on the middle small peg. Form the wire on the pattern, leaving some slack so it looks more like a heart with soft, round edges **b**. Make a second loop the same size as the first around the middle peg, stacked on top of the first loop **c**. Don't trim the excess wire. Remove the link from the jig. Repeat with the other 5-in. wire pieces.

Shape the links
Use chainnose pliers to pinch the center loops together **d**. Use chainnose pliers to bend the excess wire at the joint so it's above the loops and centered in the heart shape **e**.

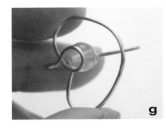

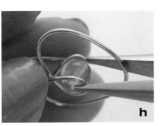

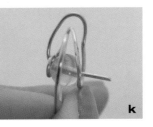

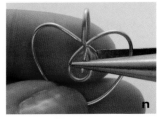

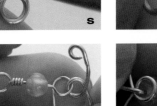

Place open roundnose pliers across the top of the heart. With your fingers, bend the wire over one jaw of the pliers, so it curves to the back of the link **f**.

Slightly adjust the loops on the front and back of the link to fit the bead.

Add the beads
Place a bead in the basket created by the center loops **g**. Adjust the fit by squeezing the loops with chainnose pliers **h**. The bead should fit snugly in the center of the link, with the holes centered in the loops.

Use chainnose pliers to make a slight bend in the wire above the bead's hole **i**.

Gently curve the wire with chainnose pliers so the wire is aligned with the bead's hole. Tuck the end of the wire into the hole of the bead **j**. Spin the bead to make it easier to slip in the wire. Slip the wire into the bead's hole and spin the bead to make it easier to push the wire through. Make a slight bend in the wire in front of the bead so the wire is flush with the bead and link **k**. Gently squeeze the link with chainnose pliers for a snug fit **l**.

With chainnose pliers, bend the wire end up toward the point where the link wires cross **m**. Squeeze the wire against the bead toward the joint **n**. Trim the excess wire that extends past the joint **o**. Squeeze the wire tail to tuck it into the joint.

Adjust the link as needed, so it is symmetrical. Make sure the large loops and the top center loop are straight **p**.

Assemble the bracelet
Connect the heart links with wrapped bead links (p. 24), modified as follows: Mark your roundnose pliers ⅜ in. (9.5mm) from the tip and form a loop 1 in. (25.5mm) from the end of a piece of 24-gauge wire, and use the new mark for the loops. Connect the loop to the top center loop on a heart link and complete the wraps. Connect the second wrapped loop to the point of another heart link. Turn the second loop perpendicular with chainnose pliers **q**. Repeat to connect all the heart links with wrapped loop bead links.

Make the toggle and finish the bracelet
Cut a 1½-in. (38mm) piece of 20-gauge wire. Form the center loop just below the tip of your roundnose pliers **r**. Form the loops on the end of the wire with the tip of your roundnose pliers so the loops turn in towards the center loop. Make a slight bend on each arm of the toggle with roundnose pliers **s, t**.

Connect the toggle to an end heart link with a wrapped bead link **u**. The heart link on the other end becomes the eye **v**.

Form Shaping Links

A mandrel is an object used to shape metal. Almost anything can be used as one. Similar to the pegs on a jig, wire is wrapped around a form to give it shape. This chapter uses a metal ring mandrel and a pen barrel as its forms. Some of these projects use a basic ring shape. Other projects modify that shape into a whole new aesthetic. A vise works in tandem with the forms, holding them steady while you shape and manipulate the wire. Use a necklace bust to help with finishing the necklace projects. The links are long and need to be curved on the form to better fit the body; this removes any jagged lines that disrupt the flow. If you don't have a necklace bust, you can make adjustments while wearing the pieces as you look in the mirror. That said, it's much easier and worthwhile to have a bust if you like making this type of jewelry.

The first projects in this chapter are based on making coils on a mandrel. The middle projects form links with a wrapped loop on a mandrel. The last two ring projects have to do with manipulating wire before it's shaped on a mandrel.

This necklace uses twisted-wire coils to add texture and whimsy to a traditional strand of pearls. You'll slip a four-pearl large bead link into the twisted spiral. The layers of materials and textures bring lots of movement to this piece.

Materials
- 22-gauge silver wire, dead-soft
- 24-gauge silver wire, dead-soft
- 32 7x9mm vertically drilled pink pearls

Tools
- chainnose pliers
- roundnose pliers
- cutters
- ruler
- pen barrel
- chasing hammer
- bench block

Make ahead
- 7 22-gauge silver wire 7x9mm pearl bead links

Twist the wire
Cut five 15-in. (38.1cm) pieces of 24-gauge wire. Twist each until it measures 6¾ in. (17.1cm) (p. 19). Cut the twisted wire into five 5¾-in. (14.6cm) pieces.

Form the four-pearl bead link
Using 22-gauge wire, make a four-pearl bead link (p. 22) **a**. Repeat to make a total of five bead links. Hammer the loops on all the bead links.

Using roundnose pliers (on Mark 2), form a loop with a 5¾-in. piece of twisted wire **b**. Hold the loop behind the pen barrel (facing left), and form a spiral around the pen **c, d**. Form a second loop on Mark 2 on the end of the wire facing in toward the center of the spiral. Clamp the loop with chainnose pliers and align the loop with the spiral **e**. Repeat with the remaining pieces of cut, twisted wire.

Slide a large bead link into the center of a twisted spiral. Open the loop on the bead link with chainnose pliers, and connect it to the adjacent loop on the spiral **f**. Stretch the spiral, making sure it's evenly spaced **g**. Open the bead link's loop on the opposite end and connect the other end of the spiral **h**. Put a slight bend in the spiral bead by gently curving it with your fingers, as shown **i**. Repeat for a total of five spiral bead links.

Make the clasp
Twist a 12-in. (30.5cm) piece of 22-gauge wire until it is 5½ in. (14cm) long. Follow the 20-gauge wire guide and make a wrapped-loop hook with non-perpendicular loops (p. 28) and a wrapped-loop eye with perpendicular loops (p. 28) out of the twisted wire.

Assemble the necklace
With chainnose pliers, open a loop on the single-pearl bead link and attach it to a twisted wire loop on a spiral bead link **j**. Repeat to connect the remaining spiral bead links with single bead links until all the pieces are connected.

Attach the hook to the loop of the end four-bead link **k**, and the eye to the end four-bead link at the other end of the chain.

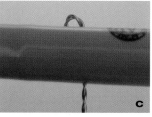

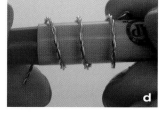

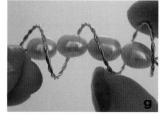

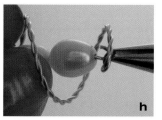

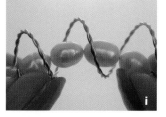

Coil and hammer wire around the ring mandrel to form these rings. Use a pebbled bead to close the gap. Make as many rings as you like, with different stones or the same stones. These rings carry the most impact when worn in multiples. The next two projects in this chapter are based on these rings.

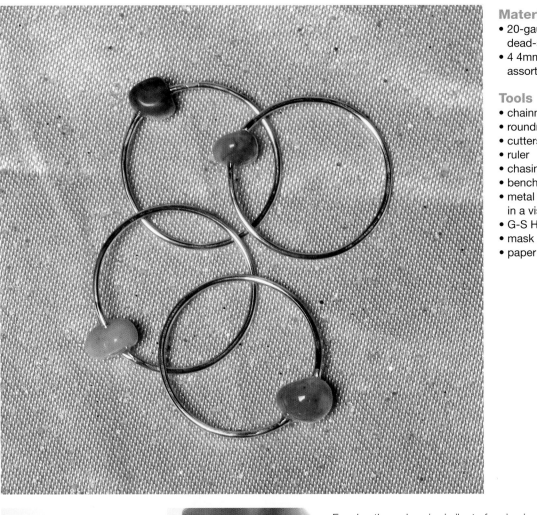

Materials
- 20-gauge silver wire, dead-soft
- 4 4mm pebble chips in assorted colors

Tools
- chainnose pliers
- roundnose pliers
- cutters
- ruler
- chasing hammer
- bench block
- metal ring mandrel secured in a vise
- G-S Hypo cement
- mask
- paper

Forming these rings is similar to forming jump-rings. Cut one 10-in. (25.4cm) piece of wire for up to a size 6 ring. Add 1 in. (25.5mm) of wire for each size larger. Using the mandrel as a guide, form a coil one size smaller than the desired finished size. With one hand, hold the end of the wire in place on the mandrel **a**. With the other hand, wrap the wire away from you a few times. With the wrapping hand, hold the coiled wire on the mandrel and with the other hand, hammer the top of the coils to work harden **b**. Move the coils over so they are all formed on the same size. Wrap the wire two more times and hammer again. Finish coiling and hammer the top of the wire. Now turn the coil and hammer it on all sides to work harden and for texture. You will still need to hold the wire to do this.

Take the coil off the mandrel and check to make sure the coils are all the same size **c**. If some are too big, twist them tighter, put them back on the mandrel, and hammer again. If some are too small, twist them larger, put them back on the mandrel, and hammer again. The coil will not fit snugly on the designated mandrel size. Just make sure that all the rings are the same size.

Cut four rings from the coil, similar to forming jump rings (p. 20) **d**. Close the links **e**.

On the bench block, press your finger onto the opening of the link and hammer the ring a few times to flatten slightly and add texture **f**. Take your finger off and gently hammer the opening once or twice. Don't hammer the opening too much, or it will be difficult to put the bead on.

Make sure the link is still a circle. If not, put it back on the mandrel and tap it a few times with the hammer. The link really won't need any heavy hammering on the mandrel to get it back to the correct shape. Repeat, if necessary, with all the rings.

Make sure the wire end of each ring fits into a bead. If not, pick out a new bead or ream the hole larger. On a piece of paper (to protect the table from any glue drips) open a ring and put a bead onto the left wire end **g**. Fit the right wire end into the bead hole **h**. Fill both sides of the hole with glue **i**. Let the ring dry on the paper for a few hours or overnight. Repeat with the remaining rings and beads. If the fumes from the glue are too strong, attach the beads in a number of sittings. If some beads are still loose, reapply the glue and let dry.

NOTE: The instructions are for ring size 6. Increase the length of the wire for larger sizes.

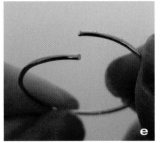

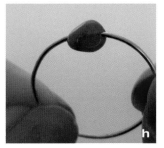

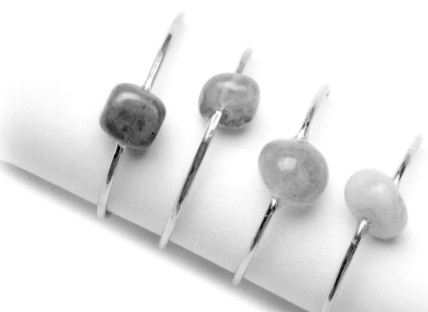

The circle links on this bracelet are formed on a pen barrel. Similar to Stack Rings, these circles are cut off the coil and finished with a bead. To add even more interest, the small circles and links are hammered flat. The flatness gives a new feeling to the wire. The hook is enlarged to match with the round links. The jagged coral chips – in contrast to the smooth metal – make a modern statement.

Materials
- 20-gauge gold wire, dead-soft
- 11 bead chips, coral

Tools
- chainnose pliers
- roundnose pliers
- cutters
- ruler
- pen secured in a vise
- chasing hammer
- bench block
- G-S Hypo cement
- mask
- paper

Make ahead
- 10 20-gauge gold S-links (p. 21)

Cut a 16-in. (40.6cm) length of 20-gauge wire.

Tightly coil the wire around the base of the pen **a**. Remove the coil from the pen, and make sure the coils are all the same size. Adjust, if necessary.

Cut 10 rings from the coil, similar to forming jump rings (p. 20) **b**. Close the rings **c**.

Hammer each ring and each S-link to flatten and to add texture. When hammering a ring, hold the open part with your fingertip to help keep the shape **d**. Watch out for your finger – these are small! Take your finger off and gently hammer the opening once or twice. Don't hammer the opening too much, or it will be difficult to put a bead on.

Make sure a bead chip fits on each ring. If not, pick out a new chip or ream the hole larger. On a piece of paper (to protect the table from glue drips), open a circle link and put a bead chip onto the left wire end **e**. Tuck the right wire end into the bead hole. Fill both sides of the hole with glue **f**. Let the ring dry on the paper for a few hours or overnight. Repeat with the remaining rings. If the fumes from the glue are too strong, attach the beads in a number of sittings. If some beads are still loose, reapply the glue and let sit until dry.

Form a hook out of 20-gauge gold wire **g** similar to a regular hook (p. 26), but trim the wire 2 in. (51mm) long and shape the hook's curve around the base of the pen. Hammer the hook to flatten, and turn the loop perpendicular.

Connect the rings with S-links **h**, alternating the beads on either side of the S-links **i**. Connect the hook to the first ring **j**. The other end ring becomes the eye.

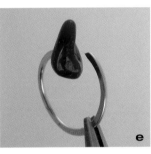
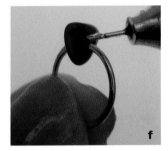

Different-sized rings connect to form this delicate necklace. The links spin, which is one of the many things I love about it. When putting it on, hold the toggle end and try to untwist the links. Flip the circles until you are happy with how it looks. The links won't lie flat, but that's part of the appeal.

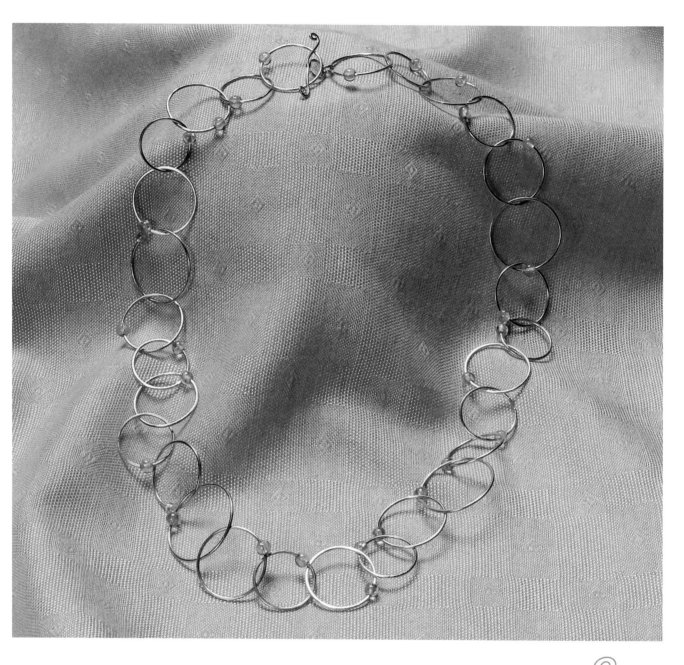

Materials
- 20-gauge gold wire, dead-soft
- 29 4mm round beads, peridot

Tools
- chainnose pliers
- roundnose pliers
- cutters
- ruler
- chasing hammer
- bench block
- metal ring mandrel secured in a vise
- G-S Hypo cement
- mask
- paper

Make ahead
- 20-gauge gold toggle (p. 27)
- 20-gauge gold jump ring (p. 20)

NOTE: I connect only five or six beads at a time because the glue fumes are very strong. I wash any glue off my fingers and take a break for 10-15 minutes. This break is also helpful in letting the glue harden. When the chain is resting, make sure the beads aren't touching any other links, or they might get glued to each other.

Form the coils
Cut two 9-in. (22.9cm) and four 10-in. (25.4cm) lengths of wire.

Refer to Stack Rings, p. 66, as you work. Incorporate these changes: form two coils on size 1 with the 9-in. lengths of wire. Form three coils on size 4 with the 10-in. lengths of wire. Form one coil on size 7 with a 10-in. length of wire.

Cut and hammer the rings
With wire cutters, cut the rings from the coil, as when making jump rings (p. 20) as follows: Cut five size 1 and 4 rings, and four size 7 rings. With chainnose pliers, close the rings and check for shape (it should be a circle). Keep the sizes separate from each other **a**.

On the bench block, hold the opening of the link with your finger and hammer the ring a few times to flatten slightly **b**. Remove your finger and gently hammer the opening once or twice. Don't hammer the opening too much, or it will be difficult to put your bead on. Make sure the link is still a circle **c**. If not, put it back on the mandrel and tap it a few times with the hammer. The link really won't need any heavy hammering on the mandrel to get it back to the correct shape. Repeat with all the rings **d**. Keep the sizes separated to avoid confusion.

TIP: Check that all your beads fit onto your rings before assembling the necklace. If some are too small, I find it easier to ream those beads before assembling **e**, **f**.

Assemble the necklace
Open a size 4 ring and put a bead onto the left wire end. Tuck the right wire end into the bead hole. Fill both sides of the hole with glue **g**, **h**, **i**. Open a size 7 ring and connect it to the size 4 bead ring. Tuck the ends into a bead hole and glue the bead in place. Repeat the linking process, gluing beads in place as you go, to form a chain with bead rings in the following order: 4, 7, 4, 1, 4, 1.

After the chain is completed, let it cure overnight. If some beads are still loose, reapply the glue and let sit until dry.

Attach the toggle to one end of the chain with a jump ring **j**. The end ring on the other end of the chain becomes the eye clasp **k**.

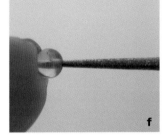

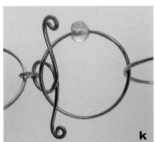

Wrapped-loop rings such as these are so versatile that the possible combinations of sizes, numbers, and accent beads are endless. These earring styles are easy to make and can be casual or dressy. Make sure to add texture to the rings with the hammer; otherwise, they are too plain.

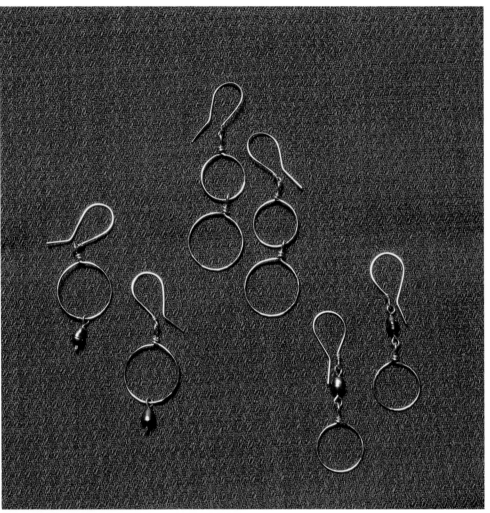

Materials
- 20-gauge dead-soft wire
- 2 2x3mm vertically drilled rice pearls

Tools
- 2 pairs of chainnose pliers
- roundnose pliers
- cutters
- ruler
- mandrel
- vise
- hammer
- bench block

Make ahead
- ear hooks (p. 29)

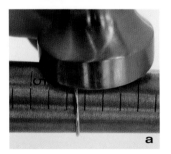

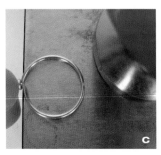

Cut a 3-in. (76mm) piece of wire.

Form a coil on size 5 of the mandrel and hammer the coil **a**. Make a perpendicular bend ⅜ in. (9.5mm) from one wire end. Tightly wrap the other wire around the bent wire two times **b**. Trim the excess wrapping wire and squeeze the wraps together with chainnose pliers. Make a link loop on Mark 2 of your roundnose pliers above the wrap. Hammer the ring on the bench block **c**, avoiding the wraps.

Make a pearl headpin, a bead link, or another ring link. Connect the loop on the ring to the ear hook with the bead link **d**.

Optional designs include attaching a pearl headpin to the ring, shown above left, or linking two rings, above center.

I have to give credit where credit is due – my husband came up with the idea of adding the beads before forming the link loop. I love to wear this necklace out to dinner. The rings are hammered flat and textured to give weight to the necklace. You can change the beads for a different look.

Materials
- 20-gauge silver wire, dead-soft
- 9 5mm round beads, African turquoise
- 9 4mm round beads, African turquoise

Tools
- 2 pairs of chainnose pliers
- roundnose pliers
- cutters
- ruler
- metal ring mandrel secured in a vise
- chasing hammer
- bench block

Make ahead
- 20-gauge silver large-wrapped-loop hook with perpendicular loop (see Coral Circles Bracelet, p. 68)
- 20-gauge silver wrapped-loop eye with non-perpendicular loop (p. 28)

Cut nine 3¾-in. (95mm) and nine 3-in. (76mm) pieces of 20-gauge wire.

Use the 3-in. pieces of wire to form wrapped loop rings on size 1 of the ring mandrel, make two wraps, and trim the excess wire.

Pinch down the wire end of the wrap with chainnose pliers. Flatten the link just below the wrapped section by clamping with chainnose pliers **a**.

Slide a 4mm bead on the wire and trim the wire to ⅜ (9.5mm) above the bead **b**. Form a loop perpendicular to the ring on Mark 2 of your roundnose pliers **c**.

Use a 3¾-in. piece of wire to form a wrapped loop ring on size 7½ of the ring mandrel, wrap twice, and trim the excess wire. Clamp down the wrapped wire ends with chainnose pliers. Slide a 5mm bead on the wire and trim the wire to ⅜ in. (9.5mm) above the bead. Form a loop perpendicular to the ring on Mark 2 of your roundnose pliers. Repeat to make nine rings.

Hammer each ring link to flatten and to add texture, avoiding the wrapped section and bead. Put each ring back on the mandrel and lightly hammer the edges for texture.

Open the loops on the wrapped loop rings and connect them, alternating between large and small **d**. Attach the hook to one end of the chain **e** and the eye to the other **f**.

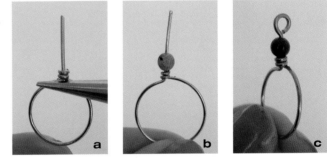

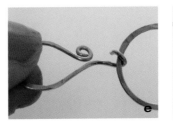

This contemporary necklace is formed on the ring mandrel and accented with wire-wrapped beads. After forming a link, bend it over the ring mandrel to better fit the body and to give the necklace a more sculptural feel. When adding the curve to the link, do so gently and slowly or it may kink.

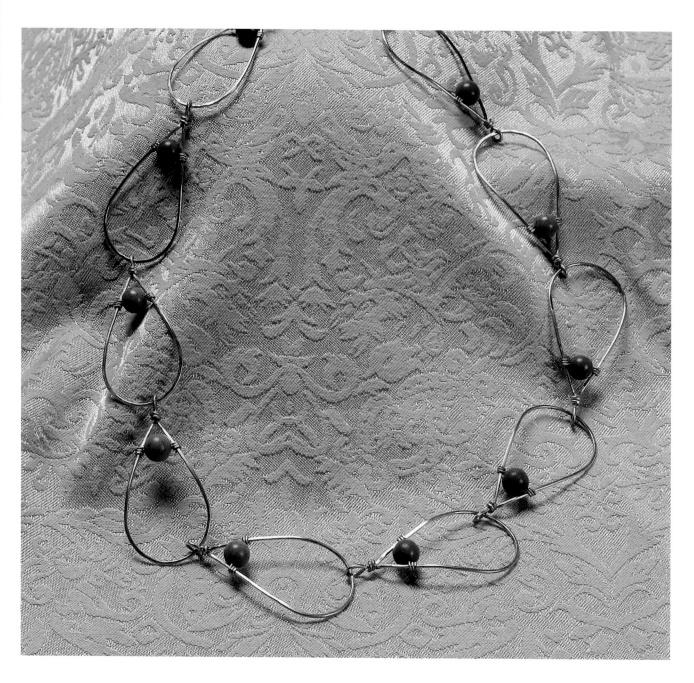

Materials
• 20-gauge silver wire, dead-soft
• 24-gauge silver wire, dead-soft
• 10 6mm round beads, turquoise

Tools
• 2 pairs of chainnose pliers
• roundnose pliers
• cutters
• ruler
• metal ring mandrel
• vise
• chasing hammer
• bench block
• necklace form

Make ahead
• wrapped-loop hook with non-perpendicular loop (p. 28)
• wrapped-loop eye with perpendicular loop (p. 28)

Cut 10 4-in. (10.2cm) pieces of 20-gauge wire and 10 2-in. (51mm) pieces of 24-gauge wire.

Secure the ring mandrel in the vise. Center a piece of 20-gauge wire at size 7 on the ring mandrel and form a teardrop shape, as shown. Adjust as needed to make it symmetrical **a**. Remove the drop from the mandrel.

Make bends in the wires ⅜-in. (9.5mm) from the ends so the wires are perpendicular to each other where they cross **b**. With chain-nose pliers, wrap the perpendicular wire around the straight wire where they cross **c**. Straighten the side of the teardrop by clamping with chainnose pliers. Form a loop using Mark 2 on your roundnose pliers above the wrap.

Hammer the link and the loop on the bench block to flatten **d**, **e**, avoiding the wrapped section. Place the shape back on the ring mandrel and hammer the curved part lightly for texture **f**. Repeat with the remaining 4-in. pieces of 20-gauge wire.

Using 2-in. pieces of 24-gauge wire, wrap to secure a bead in the crux of the link with three wraps (see wrapping a bead between two wires p. 30). Fit the bead snugly in the crux, keeping the wrapped wire straight. Repeat with the remaining links **g**.

Carefully so you don't kink it, gently curve a bead link on size 8 of the mandrel **h**. If it kinks, use chainnose pliers to clamp out the kinks **i**.

Connect the links as shown **j**.

Attach the hook to one end of the chain and the eye to the other end.

TIP: Put the necklace on a necklace form. Using the tip of your chainnose pliers, slightly bend the link loops in the center of the necklace to improve the circular flow **k**.

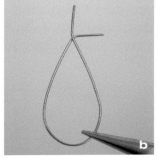

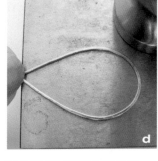

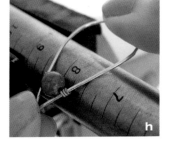

Twisted wire adds visual interest to this otherwise simple necklace. Form a wire-wrapped ring on a pen and then reshape it with chainnose pliers to form an oval. Because this twisted wire is thin, it is easy to shape. The gemstone beads on the clasp add an element of surprise.

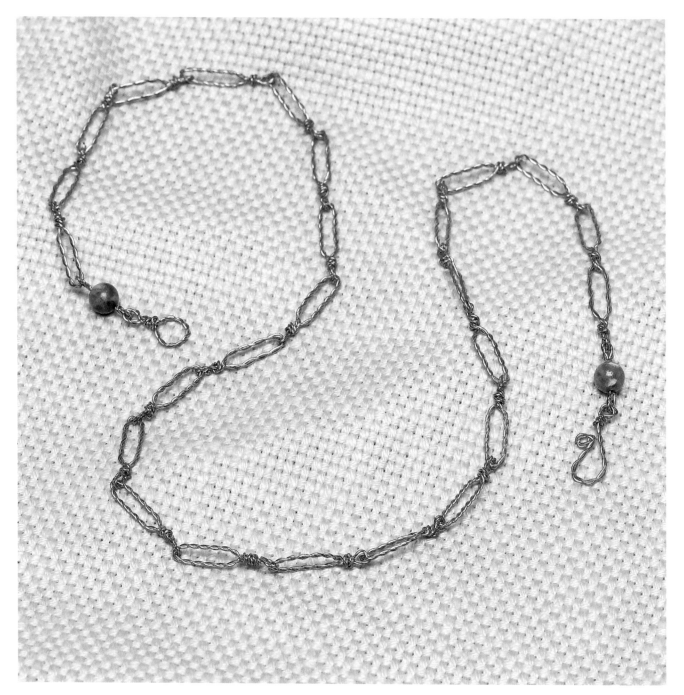

Materials
- 24-gauge copper wire
- 2 6mm round beads, sodalite

Tools
- chainnose pliers
- roundnose pliers
- cutters
- ruler
- pen secured in a vise
- chasing hammer
- bench block
- necklace form

Cut seven 21-in. (53.3cm) lengths of 24-gauge wire. Twist each segment until it is 9¾ in. (24.8cm) including the loop (p. 19).

Cut each twisted wire into four 2¼-in. (57mm) pieces. Form each 2¼-in. piece of wire into a wrapped ring, using the end of the pen barrel **a**.

With chainnose pliers, shape the ring into an oval by slowly pinching the base in the jaws of the pliers **b**. Hold the link in place with your thumbnail, just below the wrapped section. Keep the oval as symmetrical as you can. Stop when the sides bow, and straighten them by clamping with chainnose pliers **c**. Tighten the oval more by squeezing with chainnose pliers, and use the pliers to soften any edges or kinks. Flatten the link just below the wrapped section by clamping with chainnose pliers **d**.

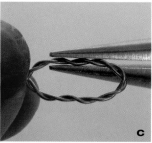

Form a link loop above the wrap, perpendicular to the ring, on Mark 2 of your roundnose pliers. If the twisted ends of the wire separate, twist them back together with chainnose pliers. To avoid separation, don't pull on the end of the wires.

Cut a 2¼-in. (64mm) piece of twisted wire from a leftover segment. Form a hook with a non-perpendicular loop following the 20-gauge wire guide (p. 26).

Cut a 2-in. (51mm) piece from the remaining 24-gauge twisted wire. Form a wrapped-loop eye with a non-perpendicular loop using the 20-gauge wire guide for measurements (p. 28).

Make two twisted wire bead links with the 6mm beads.

Hammer all the links – ovals, bead link loops, hook, and eye – to flatten.

Connect an oval ring's loop to another oval ring **e**. Repeat with all the links.

Connect the hook to one end of the chain with a 6mm bead link **f**. Connect the eye to the other end of the chain with a 6mm bead link **g**. Put the necklace on the form. Using the tip of your chainnose pliers, slightly bend the link loops above the wrapped sections in the center of the necklace to create a better circular curve **h**.

Frame pale pink pearls with hammered silver ovals. These links are formed like the twisted copper links in the preceding project. Before wrapping the pearls, make sure the ovals are wide enough to fit both the pearls and the wrapping wire.

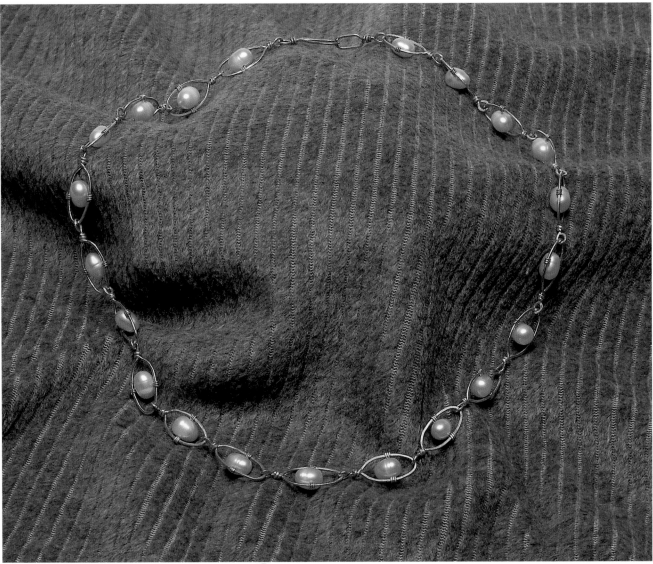

Materials
- 20-gauge silver wire, dead-soft
- 24-gauge silver wire, dead-soft
- 21 6x8mm horizontally drilled potato pearls, pale pink

Tools
- 2 pairs of chainnose pliers
- roundnose pliers
- cutters
- ruler
- pen secured in a vise
- chasing hammer
- bench block
- necklace form

Make ahead
- 20-gauge silver wire wrapped loop hook with a non-perpendicular loop (p. 28)
- 20-gauge silver wire wrapped loop eye with a non-perpendicular loop (p. 28)

Cut 21 2⅜-in. (60mm) pieces of 20-gauge wire and 21 1½-in. (38mm) pieces of 24-gauge wire.

Form wire-wrapped rings on the pen just below the cap **a**. Wrap twice and trim off any excess wire.

Using chainnose pliers, shape the ring into an oval by slowly pinching the base in the jaws of the pliers. Hold the link in place with your thumbnail just below the wrapped section **b**. Keep the oval as symmetrical as you can. Straighten any kinks in the sides by clamping with your chainnose pliers **c**. Create a more rounded oval by gently squeezing the side of the link with chainnose pliers and pushing the pliers away from the center **d**. Soften the top and bottom curve by squeezing with chainnose pliers **e**. Flatten the link just below the wrapped section by clamping with chainnose pliers **f**. Form a loop perpendicular to the ring on Mark 2 of your roundnose pliers **g**. Repeat with the remaining 2⅜-in. pieces of 20-gauge wire.

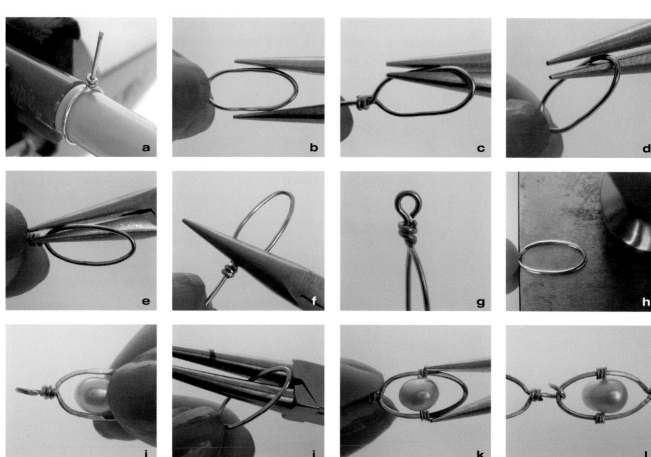

Hammer the rings and the loops to flatten, avoiding the wrapped section **h**.

Check to see that the pearl will fit into the center of the oval ring **i**. There should be a little less than a 1/16-in. (1.5mm) gap on either side of the pearl. Adjust the ring as needed by gently pulling the sides away from the center with roundnose pliers **j**. Using a 1½-in. piece of 24-gauge wire, wire wrap a pearl in the center of an oval ring with three wraps on each side of the pearl **k** (p. 30). Repeat with the remaining wrapped rings.

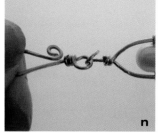

Connect the loop of a wrapped ring to the base of another wrapped ring **l**. Repeat to connect all the wrapped rings.

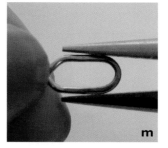

With chainnose pliers, shape the wrapped-loop eye into an oval by slowly pinching the base of the ring in the jaw of the chainnose pliers. Hold the link in place with your thumbnail just below the wrapped section **m**. Keep the oval as symmetrical as you can. Straighten any kinks in the sides by clamping them with chainnose pliers. Hammer the eye to flatten, avoiding the wrapped section.

Connect the hook to one end of the necklace **n** and the eye to the other end.

Place the necklace on the necklace form. Using the tips of your chainnose pliers, slightly bend the link loops above the wrapped section in the center of the necklace to create a curve **o**.

The band for this ring has two wrapped loops with a rectangular bead wire wrapped between the loops. Make this ring a little smaller than your normal ring size; the single-wire band is too loose otherwise.

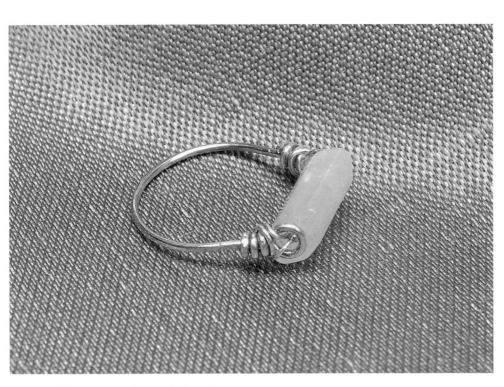

Materials
- 20-gauge silver wire, half-hard
- 24-gauge silver wire, dead-soft
- 8x10mm bead, rose quartz

Tools
- 2 pairs of chainnose pliers
- roundnose pliers
- cutters
- ruler
- metal ring mandrel secured in a vise
- chasing hammer

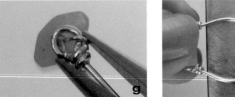

For a size 5 ring, cut a 3¼-in. (83mm) length of 20-gauge wire. Form a wrapped loop ¾ in. (19mm) from the end on each side of the wire, using Mark 2 on your roundnose pliers **a**. Wrap the wire around the mandrel, shaping it into an open ring with wrapped loops angled to each other and centered on the top of the mandrel **b**. Slightly hammer the curve of the wire on the mandrel to work harden.

Remove the ring from the mandrel and use chainnose pliers to adjust the loops, so they are facing each other **c**.

Cut one 2-in. (51mm) piece of 24-gauge wire. Hold the bead between the rings and the loops **d**. Slide the 24-gauge wire through the loop, the bead, and the other loop, leaving excess on both sides of the loops. Make a perpendicular bend on one end of the wire, next to the ring's loop to hold it in place **e**. If needed, use chainnose pliers to adjust the wrapped loops to fit more snugly to the bead. Wrap the straight wire behind the loop above the wraps. Try to keep the loop of the 24-gauge wire symmetrical. With chainnose pliers, tuck the wire end back into the bead hole **f**. Use chainnose pliers to pull the 24-gauge wire down to the wrapped section for better visual appeal **g**. Repeat on the opposite side, tightly securing the bead in place. Hammer the curve of the band on the block to work harden **h**.

SIZE GUIDE	
Sizes 6 – 6½	Cut the wire 3½ in. (89mm). Start forming the ring on size 5½. Hammer and shape to the size needed.
Sizes 7 – 7½	Cut the wire 3¾ in. (95mm). Start forming the ring on size 6½. Hammer and shape to the size needed.

This ring combines form shaping and hand shaping. The wire is doubled, wrapped, and then shaped on a whole size on the mandrel to form the band. For a half size, the band will have more texture because it is enlarged by hammering.

Materials
- 20-gauge gold wire, dead-soft
- 8–9mm half-drilled pearl, white

Tools
- chainnose pliers
- roundnose pliers
- cutters
- ruler
- chasing hammer
- bench block
- metal ring mandrel secured in a vise
- Loctite 454
- mask

For a size 5 to 5½ ring, cut a 5¼-in. (13.3cm) length of wire.

Bend the wire in half around chainnose pliers so the bend isn't a sharp angle **a**. Make a perpendicular bend ⅜ in. (9.5mm) from one end of the wire **b**. With chainnose pliers, wrap the wire with the bend around the straight wire. Use chainnose pliers to straighten the wire above the wraps.

Using your fingers, wrap the link around the ring mandrel on the size 5 mark, forming the link into a ring shape **c**. With chainnose pliers, bend the wrapped section down **d**. Slide the ring down a few sizes on the mandrel, and position the wrapped section in the bend so it's pointing toward the bend at the other end of the link **e**.

Grasp the wrap with chainnose pliers and push down to enlarge the ring slightly. Squeeze the bend wire around the wrapped section with chainnose pliers so it fits snug around the wrapped section **f**. Firmly push down on the wrapped section and move the band toward the larger sizes until it's tight on the mandrel.

Hammer the ring on the mandrel to harden, add texture, and enlarge. When hammering, spin the ring on the mandrel and hammer all the way around the ring. Remove the wrapped loop ring from the mandrel, flip it and position it on the mandrel at the mark for the desired size and hammer it again so it's symmetrical. Hammer to the whole or half size needed. If you are making a whole size, don't hammer the ring too much.

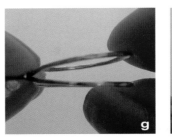

Remove the band from the mandrel, and pinch it so there is a ¼-in. (6.5mm) gap between the center of the rings **g**. Trim the straight wire to measure ⅛ in. (3mm) **h**. Clamp down the wrapped section tightly to the straight wire with the chainnose pliers.

Place the pearl on the wire, flush with the wrapped section. Trim the wire if needed. Fill the bead hole with glue and put the pearl back onto the wire **i**. Hold it in place for a minute, and then let it cure on the mandrel for a few hours or overnight.

SIZE GUIDE

Sizes 6 – 6½	Cut the wire 5½ in. (14cm). Start forming the ring on size 5½. Hammer and shape to the size needed.
Sizes 7 – 7½	Cut the wire 5¾ in. (14.6cm). Start forming the ring on size 6½. Hammer and shape to the size needed.

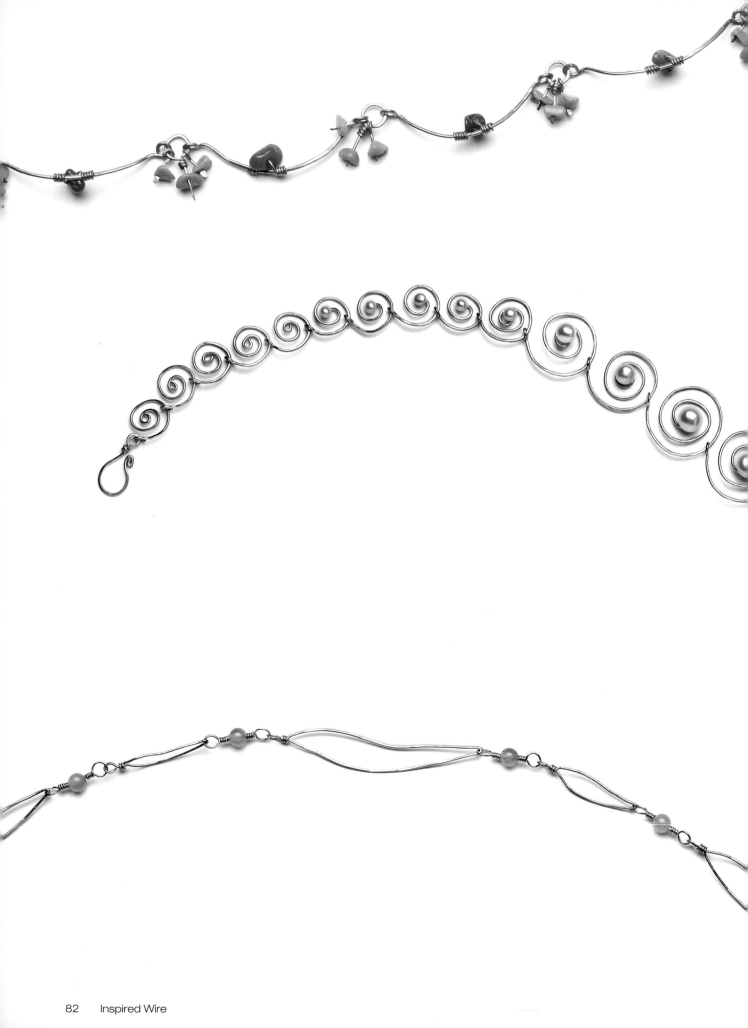

Hand Shaping Links

You'll need only your hands and your pliers to shape the pieces in this chapter. With a thorough understanding of wire and its properties, you can complete these projects. You'll find that all of the projects and techniques from the previous chapters culminate in these more complicated pieces. Since no form is used to make the jewelry in this chapter, your fingers and your eyes become your only guides.

The chapter begins with projects using links with wrapped loops. Projects with more free-formed lines follow. Finally, you'll combine these styles and add a fair amount of manipulation to form sculptural pieces.

Asymmetrical links accented by wire-wrapped beads make up these fun yet sophisticated earrings. I like the pair to be slightly different because that adds to their minimal feel. Wire wrapping and a link loop hold the link together. The next project, Falling Leaves Necklace, is based on these earrings.

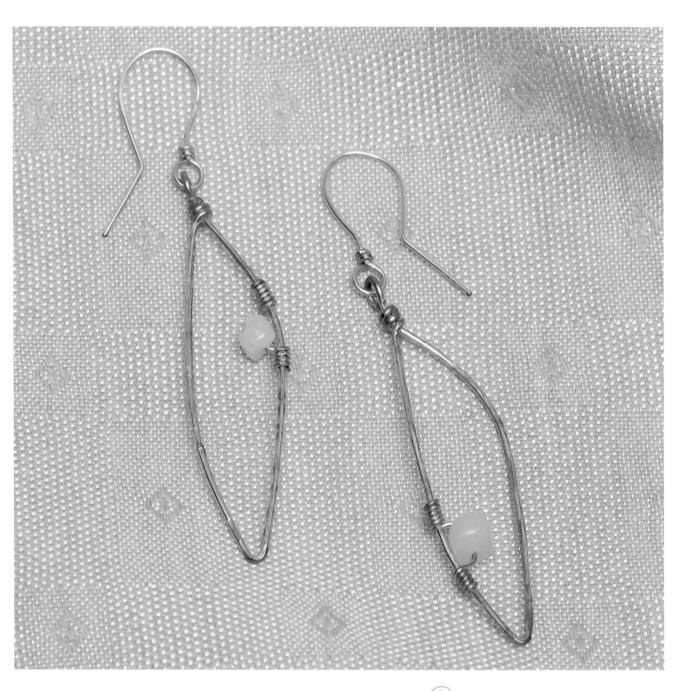

Materials
- 20-gauge gold wire, dead-soft
- 24-gauge gold wire, dead-soft
- 2 4–5mm pebble nugget beads

Tools
- 2 pairs of chainnose pliers
- roundnose pliers
- cutters
- ruler
- chasing hammer
- bench block

Make ahead
- Pair of gold wrapped-loop ear hooks with non-perpendicular loops (p. 30)

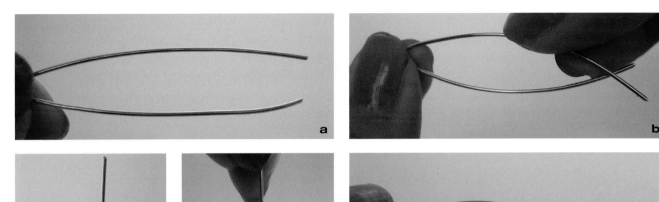

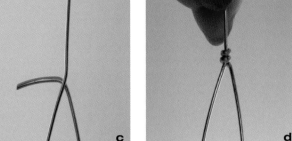

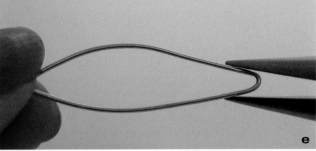

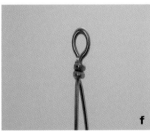

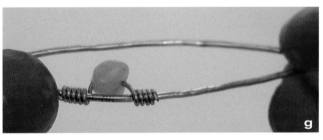

Cut two 4-in. (10.2cm) lengths of 20-gauge wire and two 2-in. (51mm) lengths of 24-gauge wire.

Using chainnose pliers, bend a 4-in. piece of wire in half so it resembles a slim "V" **a**. Hold the tip of the "V" in one hand, and pinch one side of the wire with your thumb and forefinger **b**. Curve the wire with your fingers by pulling and pinching in a downward motion.

Bend both wires ⅜-in. (9.5mm) from the ends so the wires are perpendicular. Curve the link slightly so the bends on the wires cross **c**. Wrap the bent wire around the straight wire two times. Trim the excess wrapping wire **d**. Squeeze the point of the link with chainnose pliers **e**. With your fingers, shape the link by pushing out on the longer side to create a pea pod shape. Make a link loop above the wraps on Mark 2 of your roundnose pliers **f**. Repeat these two steps with the remaining piece of 20-gauge wire to make a second link.

Hammer both links and loop on the bench block to flatten, avoiding the wrapped section.

Slide a bead to the center of a piece of 24-gauge wire and wrap the bead to the top curve with five wraps on each side of the bead (p. 31) **g**. Don't forget to tightly clamp down the wrapped wire to flatten with chainnose pliers **h**.

Attach a link to each ear hook **i**.

NOTE: I find the earrings more interesting if they aren't mirror images of each other.

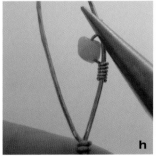

Large and small leaf shapes are made to delicately circle the neck. The thin wire used to make the leaves is strengthened by a lot of manipulation and hammering. The thinner wire also gives you the option for more bends and curves when shaping. As you form each leaf, try to give it plenty of texture and character for a more organic effect. Since the links are long, the piece needs to be put on a necklace bust and shaped to match the curves of neck, shoulders, and collarbone.

Materials
- 22-gauge gold wire, dead-soft
- 24-gauge gold wire, dead-soft
- 9 5mm round beads, green garnet

Tools
- 2 pairs of chainnose pliers
- roundnose pliers
- wire cutters
- ruler
- chasing hammer
- bench block
- necklace form

Make ahead

- 22-gauge gold wrapped-loop hook with perpendicular loop (p. 28)
- 22-gauge gold wrapped-loop eye with perpendicular loop (p. 28)

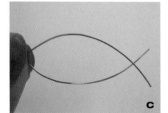
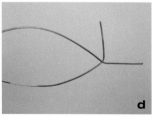
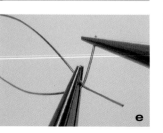
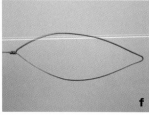

Cut four 4¾-in. (12.1cm) and five 2¾-in. (70mm) pieces of 22-gauge wire. Cut six pieces of 2⅛ in. (54mm) 24-gauge wire.

Form the large leaf links
Using chainnose pliers, bend a piece of 4½ in. (11.4cm) wire just to the left of the center to form a "V" **a**. Hold the tip of the "V" in one hand, and pinch one side of the wire with your thumb and forefinger. Curve the wire by pulling and pinching in a downward motion **b, c**. Measure ⅜ in. (9.5mm) on the end of the wire and bend one end perpendicular to the other. The bends should touch each other **d**. Wrap the bent wire around the straight wire with chainnose pliers **e, f**.

With your fingers, squeeze and shape the link to curve inward slightly – push the short side to the longer side about ¼ in. (6.5mm) at the widest area **g**. The widest part of the link should be closer to the wrapped loop and not the point. Squeeze the tip of the link with chainnose pliers to a smaller point **h**. Straighten any kinks in the wire, especially near the point, with chainnose pliers. Adjust the wire until you are happy with the shape. (See **i** for the approximate size and shape.) Form a link loop facing back on the straight wire on Mark 1 of your roundnose pliers **j, k**.

Repeat the "Form the large leaf links" steps with the remaining 4½-in. wires.

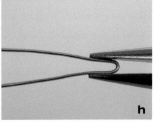

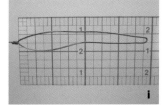

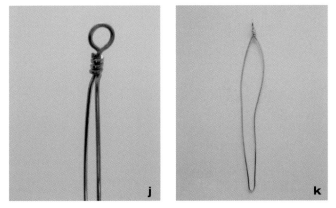

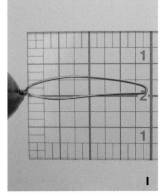

Form the small leaf links

Repeat "Form the large leaf links" using 2¾-in. (70mm) lengths of wire **l**, **m**.

On the bench block, hammer the link and loop of all the leaf links to flatten and to add texture, avoiding the wrapped sections **n**.

Form the chain

Measure in 5⁄16 in. (8mm) from the tip of your roundnose pliers, and mark it with a pen. Make a perpendicular bend ⅞ in. (22mm) from the end of a piece of 2⅛ in. (54mm) 24-gauge wire. Form a wrapped loop using the new mark on the roundnose pliers, wrapping four times (p. 23) **o**. Slide a bead on the wire and bend the wire 1⁄16 in. above the bead with chainnose pliers. Cut the wire ⅞ in. from the bend and form the beginning of a wrapped loop; then connect it to the tip of a small leaf **p**. Make four wraps and trim the excess wire. With chainnose pliers, turn the first wrapped loop perpendicular to the one connected to the small leaf. Continue building a chain of alternating small and large leaves connected with bead links.

With bead links, connect the clasp components directly to the ends of the chain **q**.

Put the necklace on a necklace form. With your fingers, bend the leaves as needed for a better fit around the neck, shoulders, and collarbones **r, s**. On the front center of the necklace, use chainnose pliers to slightly bend the link loops above the wrapped sections to create a better flow for the chain **t**.

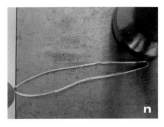

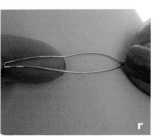

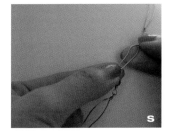

Falling Leaves Necklace

Inspired Wire　87

In this project, a ruler helps you form square twisted-wire links. Be as accurate as possible for the best looking earrings. When you're adding the wrapped beads, you may find it challenging to keep the wrapping-wire even. A trick is to constantly adjust the wrapping wire with chainnose pliers. Making adjustments during the wrapping rather than waiting until the project is completed is easier and more visually appealing.

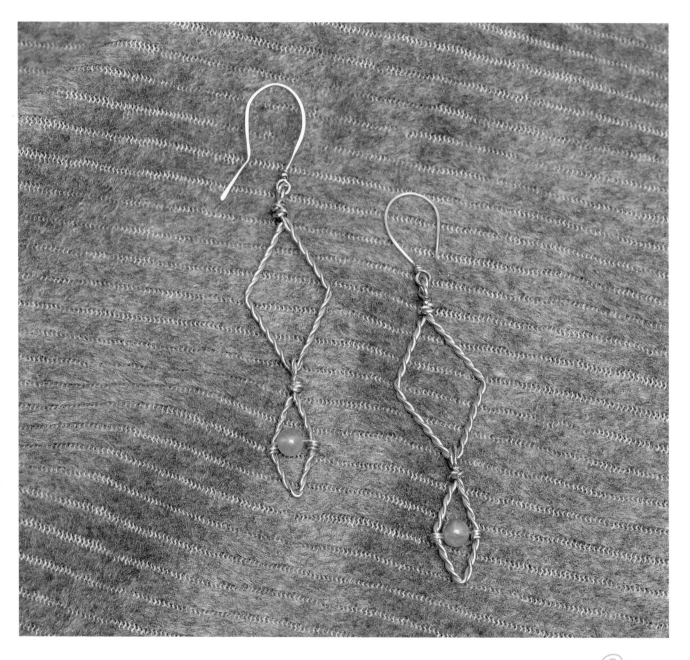

Materials
- 22-gauge silver wire, dead-soft
- 24-gauge silver wire, dead-soft
- 2 5mm round beads, green garnet

Tools
- Two pairs of chainnose pliers
- roundnose pliers
- cutters
- ruler

Make ahead
- wrapped-loop ear hooks with non-perpendicular loops (p. 30)

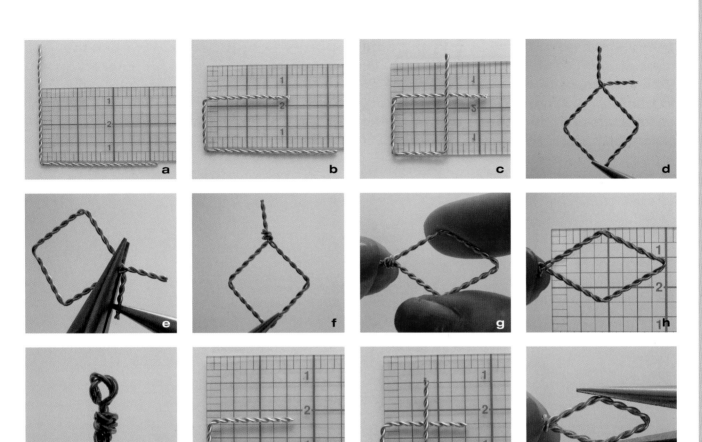

Cut two 19-in. (48.3cm) lengths of 22-gauge wire. Twist each wire in the vise until it is 8¾ in. (20.3cm) long, including the loop. Cut the twisted wire into two 3¼-in. (83mm) and two 2¼-in. (57mm) pieces.

Form the large diamonds

Using chainnose pliers, make a 90° bend in the center of a 3¼-in. piece of twisted wire (use a C-Thru ruler to get the correct angle) **a**. Measure ⅝ in. (16mm) from the bend, and make a 90° bend on each side **b, c**. Bend one wire perpendicular to the other wire **d**. Wrap the bent wire around the straight wire with chainnose pliers **e, f**.

With your fingers or chainnose pliers, squeeze the corners of the square to shape it into a diamond **g**. The diamond should measure 1 in. (25.5mm) from the bottom point to the bottom of the wrapped section and ⅝ in. from side point to side point **h**. Form a link loop above the wraps, perpendicular to the diamond, on Mark 2 of your roundnose pliers **i**. Adjust the shape with chainnose pliers to make it symmetrical. Repeat to make a second diamond with the other 3¼-in. piece of twisted wire.

Form the small diamonds

Follow the directions for "Form the large diamond," but use a 2¼-in. (57mm) piece of twisted wire. The corners on the small diamond measure ⅜ in. (9.5mm) apart **j, k**, and the small diamond is ⅝ in. (16mm) from the bottom point to the bottom of the wraps **l, m**. Repeat with the second 2¼-in. piece of twisted wire.

Complete the earrings

Cut two 1½-in. (38mm) pieces of 24-gauge wire. Secure a bead into the center of a small diamond with wraps at the diamond's right and left corners, using a piece of 24-gauge wire (p. 30). Clamp tightly with chainnose pliers to secure **n, o**. Repeat with the second small diamond.

Connect the small diamond links to the bottoms of the large diamond links **p**. Connect the large diamond links to the wrapped-loop ear hooks **q**.

These earrings are very simple and contemporary – perfect for adding just the right amount of style to a sleek outfit. One end of each earring is hammered wider than the opposite end. Since they are so simple, any flaw will show. Take your time to hammer and shape each earring to be exact copies of the other. Please be very careful when putting these on. Pinch the tip of the earring with your fingers, so the wire won't accidentally injure you.

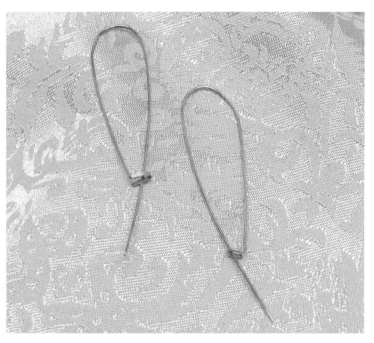

Materials
• 22-gauge silver or gold wire

Tools
• 2 pairs of chainnose pliers
• roundnose pliers
• cutters
• ruler
• chasing hammer
• bench block
• file

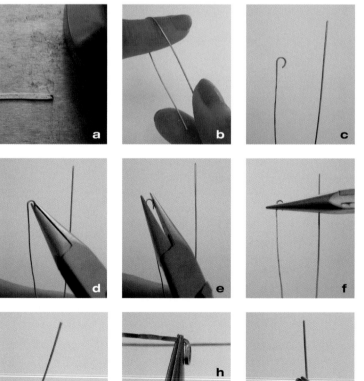

Cut a 4-in. (10.2cm) piece of wire and hammer the wire to flatten it on a bench block. On one end only, hammer it very flat for about 1 in. (25.5mm) **a**. Repeat with a second 4-in. wire.

Shape the hook by measuring in 2¼-in. (57mm) from the thinner end of the wire, and curving that spot over the side of your knuckle **b**. Remove any kinks in the wire by clamping with chainnose pliers.

Shape the catch on the shorter end by forming an open loop using Mark 1 on your roundnose pliers **c**. Use chainnose pliers to straighten the loop into a "U" **d, e**. Tighten the "U" by squeezing it with chainnose pliers **f**.

Shape a hook and catch on the second wire.

Bend the "U" toward the side with chainnose pliers **g**.

With one pair of chainnose pliers, tightly clamp the wire above the "U" **h**. With the other pair of chainnose pliers, turn the "U" so the opening faces forward **i**. Close the earrings by sliding the long wire into the U-shaped hooks. Bend the "U" to a sharp angle with chainnose pliers **j**.

File the end of the longer wire flat to round the edges and to remove all burrs. Repeat to finish the second earring. Close the earrings and make any adjustments so they are symmetrical.

The larger links for these earrings are based on the wrapped-loop eye. The clusters of bright turquoise chips create lots of movement. People can't seem to take their eyes off them! I used gold ear hooks because my ears are too sensitive for copper. If you don't have sensitive ears, feel free to use copper. Some links in the next project are based on these earrings.

Materials
- 22-gauge copper wire
- 22-gauge gold wire, half-hard
- 18 bead chips, turquoise
- 2 bead chips, coral

Tools
- 2 pairs of chainnose pliers
- roundnose pliers
- cutters
- ruler
- chasing hammer
- bench block

Make ahead
- 12 22-gauge copper head-pins with turquoise bead chips (p. 22)
- 2 gold ear hooks with non-perpendicular loops and coral bead chip slipped on before forming a hook on a pen barrel (p. 29) **a**.

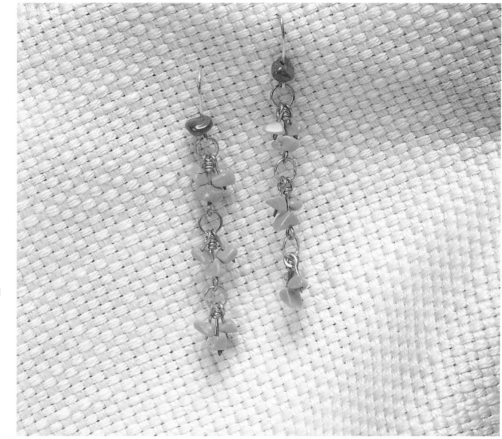

Wrapped-loop bead links (A)

Cut a 1¾-in. (44mm) piece of wire and form a large wrapped loop ⅔ of the way down the jaw of the roundnose pliers, with three wraps (p. 23). Slide a turquoise bead chip on the wire **b**, and form a link loop perpendicular to the wrapped loop **c** Repeat to make a second bead link.

Attach two turquoise headpins to either side of the wrapped loop of the bead links **d**.

Wrapped-loop headpins (B)

Cut a 1⅛-in. (29mm) piece of wire. Form a large wrapped loop ⅔ of the way down the jaw of the roundnose pliers. Slide a turquoise chip onto the wire and hammer the end of the wire to hold the chip in place. Repeat to make a second headpin.

Attach two turquoise headpins to the loop of the wrapped-loop headpin **e**.

Attach the link loop of an A link to the wrapped loop of another A link **f**. Attach the loop of the second A link to the wrapped loop of a B link. Attach an ear hook to the wrapped loop of the first A link **g**.

Repeat with the remaining materials to make a second earring.

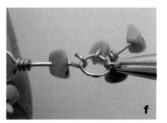

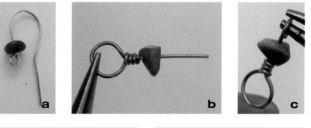

This dainty necklace can be dressed up or dressed down. There are several types of links in this necklace. For the best result, it is important to form the links as similarly as possible. Check your measurements a few times before cutting. Any measuring mistake is quite evident.

Materials
- 20-gauge copper wire
- 22-gauge copper wire
- 24-gauge copper wire
- 26 turquoise bead chips
- 9 coral bead chips

Tools
- 2 pairs of chainnose pliers
- roundnose pliers
- cutters
- ruler
- chasing hammer
- bench block

Make ahead
- 18 22-gauge copper turquoise headpins (p. 22)
- 8 22-gauge copper wrapped-loop turquoise headpins (p. 91)
- 20-gauge copper wrapped-loop hook with a non-perpendicular loop (p. 28)
- 20-gauge wrapped-loop eye with a non-perpendicular loop (p. 28)

Form the curved links

Cut nine 2-in. (51mm) pieces of 20-gauge wire and form loops toward the center of the wire on both ends, using Mark 2 of your roundnose pliers **a**. Use chainnose pliers to remove any kinks.

With your fingers and thumb, curve the links in the center **b, c**. The links should be ⅜ in. (9.5mm) long **d, e**. Hammer the links to flatten and for texture **f, g**.

Shape the link loops

Use two pairs of chainnose pliers to bend the loops of the curved links as shown **h, i, j**. Twist the loops back and then bend them perpendicular. The loops should be in a straight line with each other. The link should be ¼-in. (6.5mm) high **k**.

Add the beads

Cut nine 2-in. pieces of 24-gauge wire. Wire wrap a coral chip to the center of each curved link with 24-gauge wire (p. 31). Angle the chip forward slightly with your finger, so the link will lie flat **l, m**.

Attach two turquoise headpins to each wrapped loop headpin **n**.

Assemble the necklace

Connect the links alternating between the curved links and wrapped-loop links **o, p**. Attach the remaining turquoise headpins to the loop on the hook and the loop on the eye **q**. Attach the hook to one end of the chain, and the eye to the other **r**.

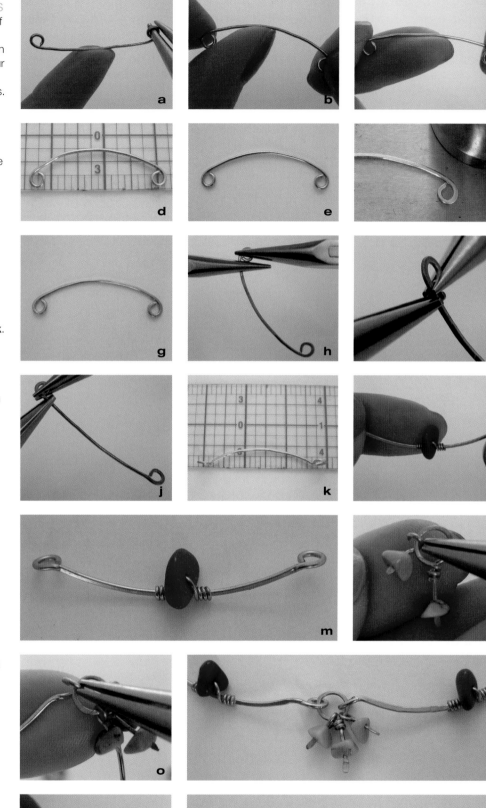

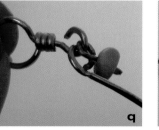

I love the organic forms in this quick bracelet. The rose quartz pebble beads lend a natural and somewhat glowing sensation. Use a vise to twist multiple lengths of wire together to form this bracelet. Add beads to each piece of wire before twisting. Take care not to twist too tightly or the beads will break and crack. The form is all in one – the eye, the body, and the hook are all part of the same wires.

Materials
- 20-gauge silver wire, dead-soft
- 16 5-6mm pebble nugget beads, rose quartz
- 4mm half-drilled bead, rose quartz

Tools
- chainnose pliers
- roundnose pliers
- cutters
- ruler
- pen
- vise
- Loctite 454

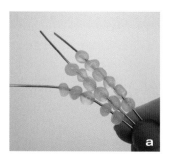

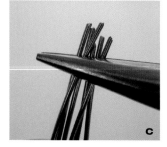

Cut three 20-in. (50.8cm) lengths of wire.

String five nuggets on two wires, and six nuggets on the remaining wire **a**. Slide the beads to the end of the wires.

Bring both ends of the wires together evenly **b**, and tightly twist the wires together for 2 in. (51mm) with chainnose pliers **c, d**. Slip the end of the twisted wires into the vise and tighten until the wires are secure **e**.

Slip the pen in the middle of the wire and pull the wire taught. Slide one bead down a wire and on the pen **f**. Space the beads with your fingers across the length of the wires **g**.

Twist the wires slowly and position the beads as desired while you twist the wires **h**. Twist until the wires are tight, but don't twist them so tight that the beads break.

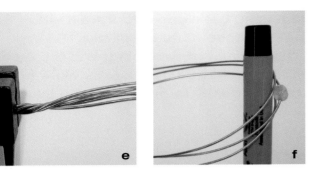

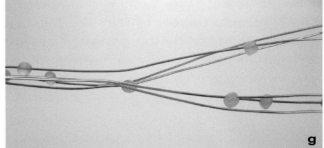

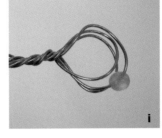

Use the loop with the bead as the eye **i**.

Trim the wires, one at a time, ¾ in. (19mm) from the end **j**. With chainnose pliers, twist the trimmed ends together tightly **k**.

Bend the ends into a hook shape with roundnose pliers **l**. Twist the ends back together with chainnose pliers, if needed.

Use the cutters to trim 1⁄16 in. (1.5mm) from the ends of five of the wires **m**.

Position the half-drilled bead on the untrimmed wire at the end of the hook **n**. The bead should be flush with the wire ends. Trim the wires if necessary. Remove the bead from the wire, fill the hole with glue, and attach it to the wire at the end of the hook. Hold it in place for a few minutes until it's secured. Let the glue dry completely.

With your fingers, curve the twisted wires to form an oval **o**. Use roundnose pliers to bend the hook back to fit into the eye **p**, and turn the hook so the beaded end is slightly pushed in toward the center of the bracelet. This makes it easier to close the clasp. Adjust the angle of the eye with chainnose pliers, if needed **q**. Hook the clasp together **r**.

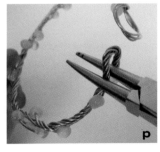

VARIATION: The gold bracelet is made with three lengths of 22-gauge wire and 4mm round beads. It's much thinner than the silver bracelet.

In this bracelet, you'll use one piece of wire for the base and decorate it with wire-wrapped beads. I really like this bracelet because of its simplicity. The style is easily changed by the gauge of the wire, the amount of wrapping, and the types of beads or combination of beads you select. Large flat-backed beads work best. The slimmer profile makes them have less of a tendency to get caught on things when being worn.

Materials
- 20-gauge silver wire, dead-soft
- 24-gauge silver wire, dead-soft
- 6 7x15mm rectangle beads, shell
- 6 8x9mm button-pearls, white

Tools
- 2 pairs of chainnose pliers
- roundnose pliers
- cutters
- ruler
- vise
- chasing hammer
- bench block

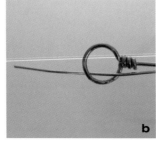

Cut a 10½-in. (26.7cm) piece of 20-gauge wire and make a large wrapped loop on one end of the wire, as follows: Bend the wire 1¼ in. (32mm) from the end and form the loop at the base of your roundnose pliers (p. 23) **a**.

Cut a 20-in. (50.8cm) piece of 24-gauge wire. Hold the two wires together so 1½ in. (38mm) of the 24-gauge wire extends past the wrapped loop **b**. Place the eye and the 24-gauge wire in the vise **c**. Bend the 24-gauge wire toward you, and tightly wrap it around the

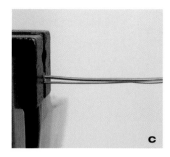

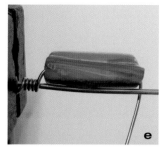

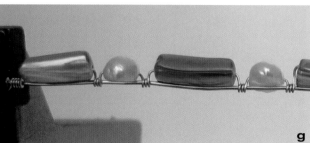

20-gauge wire four times. Push the wraps together with chainnose pliers, if necessary **d**.

Make a slight bend in the 24-gauge wire ⅛ in. (3mm) (or based on the position of the bead hole) above the wrapped section with chainnose pliers. Slide a shell bead on the 24-gauge wire **e**, bend the wire down next to the bead, and bring it behind the 20-gauge wire and make three wraps. On the same side as the bead, make a slight bend with chainnose pliers ⅛ in. above the wrapped section. Add a pearl bead and wrap three times **f**. Repeat adding beads and wrapping three times, alternating the remaining beads. After attaching every couple of beads, push them towards the vise so the coils are close to the beads. Squeeze the coils together with chainnose pliers as you wrap, too. After the last bead is slipped on **g**, wrap the 24-gauge wire four times and cut off any excess 24-gauge wire. Remove the wire from the vise. Pinch down the ends of the 24-gauge wire with chainnose pliers. Leave the excess 24-gauge wire by the eye.

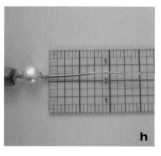

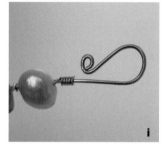

Trim the 20-gauge wire to measure 1½ in. (38mm) **h**, and form a hook with the wire (p. 26) **i, j**.

Hammer the hook and the wrapped-loop eye on the bench block to work harden.

Curve the bracelet with your fingers to form a circle **k, l**. Adjust the hook and eye so they hinge together easily. Using your fingers or chainnose pliers, bend the eye and the hook so they curve in towards each other **m**. Wrap the 24-gauge wire around the base of the eye to fill in the gap **n** and trim the excess wire. Check the fit, and adjust the angle of the clasp if needed.

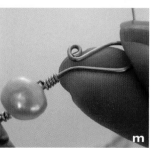

VARIATION:
This bracelet is made with 20-gauge and 24-gauge gold wire and 11 7x11mm rectangle rose quartz beads.

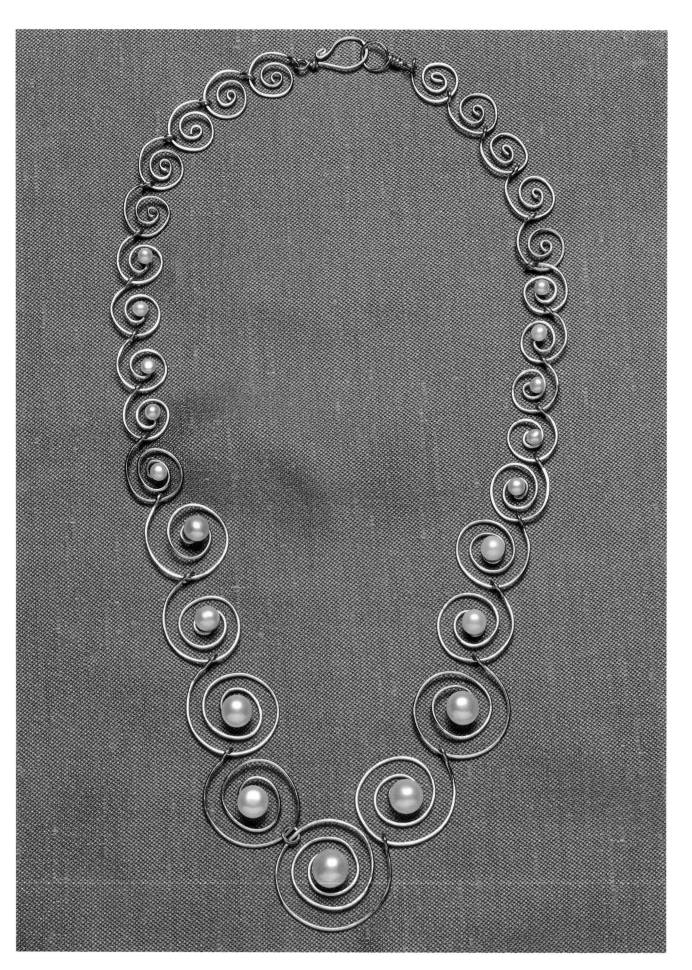

Graduated links and pearls form into a delicate and elegant necklace that perfectly drapes the neck. Equal spaces between the spirals keep them looking crisp and formal, so do your best to shape the spirals evenly. Make sure the button back pearl is firmly placed on the spiral link. Any gaps or mistakes throw off the balance of this striking piece.

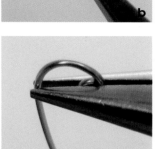

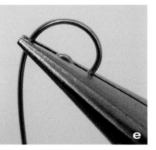

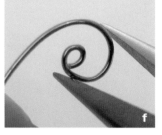

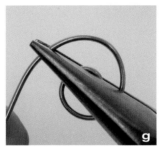

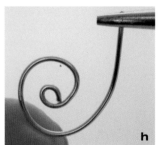

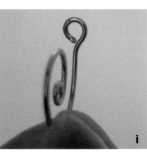

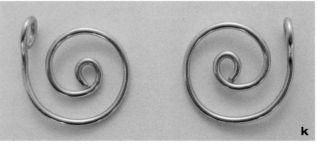

Materials
- 20-gauge gold wire, dead-soft
- 8–8.5mm half-drilled button pearl, white
- 4 7–7.5mm half-drilled button pearls, white
- 4 5–5.6mm half-drilled button pearls, white
- 10 3–3.5mm half-drilled button pearls, white

Make ahead
- 20-gauge gold wrapped-loop hook clasp formed around a pen barrel (see Coral Circles Bracelet, p. 68)
- 20-gauge gold wrapped-loop eye with a perpendicular loop (p. 28)
- jump ring made ⅓ of the way down roundnose pliers on Mark 2 (p. 20)

Tools
- 2 pairs of chainnose pliers
- roundnose pliers
- cutters
- ruler
- hammer
- block
- Loctite 454
- bead reamer
- mask

Form the spiral links

Cut the 20-gauge wire into the following lengths: 18 2¼ in. (57mm) for A and B links, two 3 in. (76mm) for C links, four 4 in. (10.2cm) for D links, four 5 in. (12.7cm) for E links, one 7 in. (17.8cm) for F link. (See the chart on p. 101 to help with spiral forming.)

Form a small loop at one end of the wire with the tip of the roundnose pliers **a**. Tighten the loop by squeezing it with chainnose pliers **b**.

Form a spiral by clamping the loop with chainnose pliers **c**, and gently roll and curve the wire around the outside of the loop to form part of the spiral **d**, **e**. Remove the wire from the pliers and adjust the shape so it is symmetrical **f**. Continue forming the spiral evenly as shown **g**.

When the spiral is almost completely formed, make a basic loop at the end on Mark 2 of your roundnose pliers **h**. Straighten the loop **i**, and curve the wire to match the shape of the spiral **j**. Make a total of 10 size A spirals, eight size B spirals, two size C spirals, four size D spirals, and four size E spirals, half with the loop on the right and half with the loops on the left **k**. Make the loop on the single size F spiral on the right.

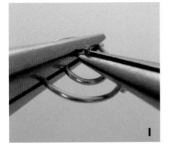

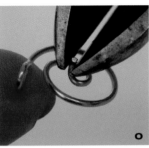

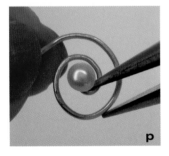

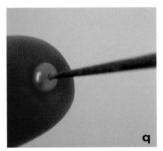

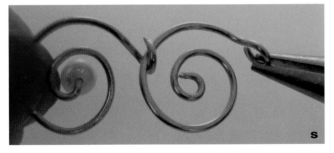

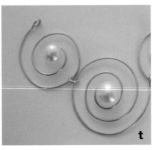

Shape the links to fit the pearls

With a pair of chainnose pliers, tightly clamp the center of the F link where the inside loop touches the spiral. With the second pair of chainnose pliers in your other hand, turn up the loop to form a shank to which the pearl will attach **l**. Adjust and straighten the shank with chainnose pliers by clamping and squeezing until it is perpendicular **m**. Repeat with the E links, D links, C links, and B links.

Hammer

On the block, hammer all the links and the jump ring to work harden and to slightly flatten. Avoid the shank and the loop as necessary. Push down the link loop over the edge of the block to avoid hitting it **n**.

Add the pearls

Using the cutters, trim the shank so the pearl will be flush with the link **o**. (The B links need to cut close to the base of the link for the pearl to be flush.) Fit the pearl and adjust the link until the pearl is centered **p**. Trim the shank more, if necessary. If the hole of the pearl is too small or not deep enough, make it larger with a bead reamer **q**. Ensure the proper fit and location of the pearl before attaching it.

With the pearl face down on your fingertip, put a small drop of glue in the hole. Firmly press the shank into the bead hole. Avoid getting the glue on your fingers or on top of the pearl. The back of the pearl should be flush with the link **r**.

Repeat with the remaining links with shanks and pearls, following the chart at the right for sizing.

Assemble the necklace

This necklace is graduated with the F link in the center. Open the loop on a link and connect to the outside spiral of the next link **s**. Start by connecting the link loop of the F link to the outside spiral of one right E link, connect that to the other right E link, then connect to two right D links, one right C link, four right B links, and five right A links.

On the other side, use the jump ring to connect the center F link with a left E link **t**. Continue the above pattern for the remainder of the side, using the left links.

Connect the hook to one side and the eye to the other side.

SIZE CHART

	Link	Quantity	Pearl size
	A	10 5 with left loops, 5 with right loops	0
	B	8 4 with left loops, 4 with right loops	3-3.5mm
	C	2 1 with left loop, 1 with right loop	3-3.5mm
	D	4 2 with left loops, 2 with right loops	5-5.5mm
	E	4 2 with left loops, 2 with right loops	7-7.5mm
	F	1 loop on right	8-8.5mm

Coral Circles necklace

Lace ring

Hera's necklace

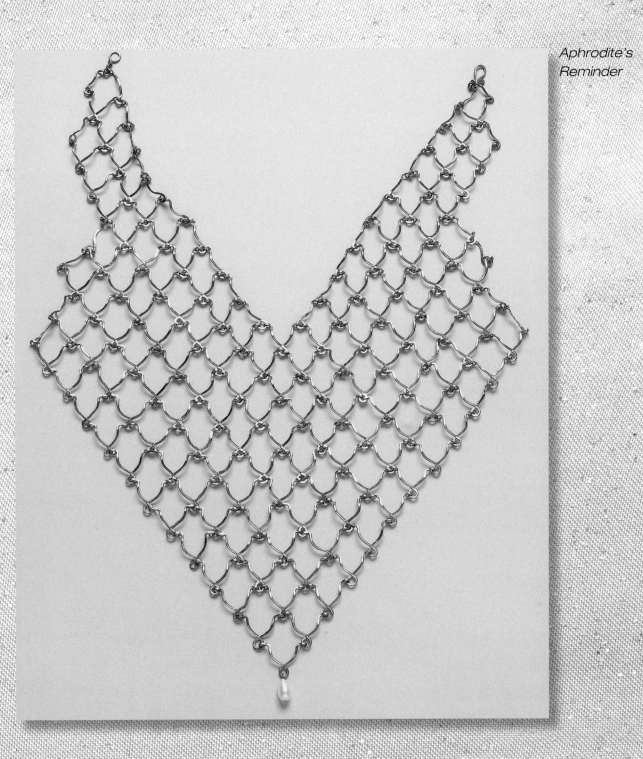

*Aphrodite's
Reminder*

Clover ring

Shell necklace

Crown ring

Rays of the Sun necklace

Wire wrap earrings

Rock Sugar earrings

Pearl Ladder earrings

Demeter's Hope
necklace, bracelet, and earrings

Turquoise Tier necklace

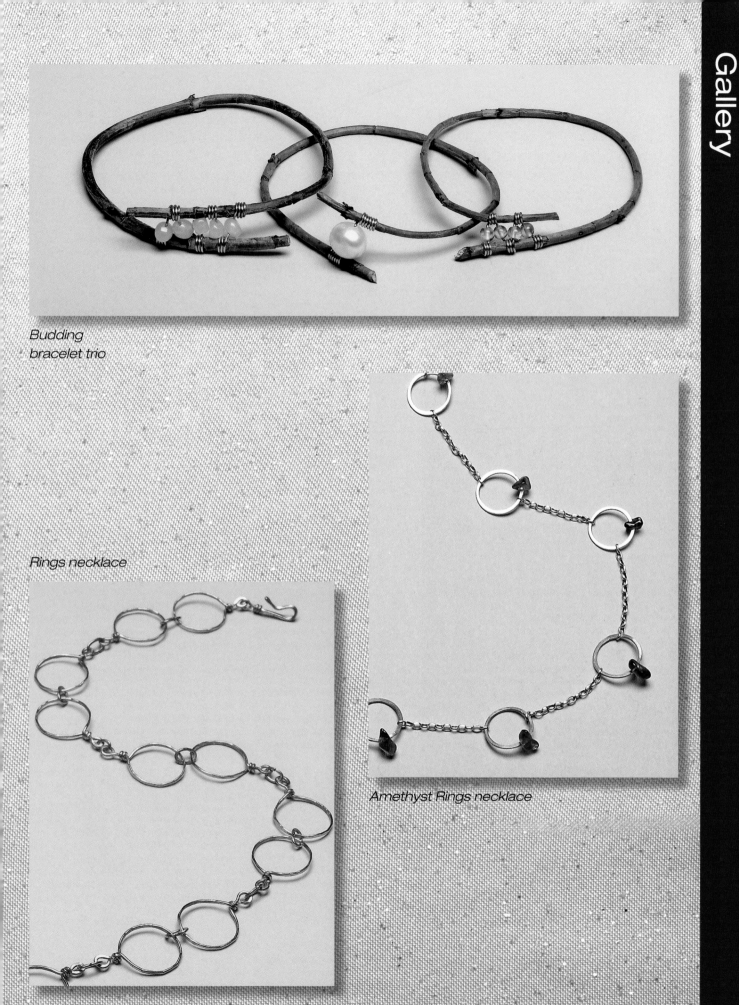

Budding
bracelet trio

Rings necklace

Amethyst Rings necklace

Conclusion

Congratulations on finishing the book! You have learned how to twist, jig, bend, hammer, and wrap. The world of wire jewelry is now at your fingertips. I hope my projects and ideas have given you a great source of inspiration for jewelry or any other type of art or design. Keep building on these techniques and learn new ones. Then combine them to make a style all your own. Thank you so much for using my book!

You've created a great collection – go out and show it off!

About the Author

Cynthia B. Wuller's love of enchanting stories has always inspired her to create works reflecting those fanciful ideals. The urge to learn and create is the basis of her well-rounded art background, which includes a Bachelor of Fine Arts from the School of the Art Institute of Chicago. Cynthia is a contributor to *Art Jewelry* and *BeadStyle* magazines. Her work can also be found in a number of books, such as *Easy Beading Volume 4*, *The Art of Jewelry: Paper Jewelry*, *The Art of Jewelry: Wood*, and *Beading with Pearls*.

Acknowledgments

I give my most sincere thanks and appreciation to every-one who helped this book come to fruition, including God for all His love, blessings, and gifts, and those in heaven who constantly are there for us, and also to:

The wonderful folks at Kalmbach:
- Pat Lantier, for helping me hold the course and keep steady
- Karin Buckingham, who started me off on the right track and then helped me through to the finish
- Salena Safranski, who made sure everything is okay
- Nanz Aalund, Jill Erickson, Katie Streeter, and Amy Robleski at *Art Jewelry,* and Linsday Haedt and Jane Konkel at *BeadStyle,* who welcomed and helped me into the world of publishing
- To everyone who worked so hard to make this book come to life

My mother and father deserve so much more than thanks and appreciation for their love, support, and guidance. They expanded my creativity, exposed me to different cultures, educated me in and about art, and constantly teach me to be me.

My husband, Miles, whose boundless and unwavering love and devotion for me gives me the time and space to create anything and everything my heart desires. Your support and interest in what I do is the backbone for everything I make.

My sister, Christina, her husband, Jonathan, and their wonderful family: Thank you for helping me choose the good and better designs and livening up my days.

Huge thanks and appreciation to my husband's parents, sister Megan, and Grandma. Your constant love, help, and encouragement mean so much to me. I love sharing all my thoughts and dreams with you.

I'm grateful for our family and friends, including Aunt Aurora and Uncle Bill, Teresita, David, Suzanne, Hannah, Virginia, and Fr. Dowd. Knowing I have such wonderful people supporting and helping me makes me feel so blessed and thankful.

A special thanks to Table Top Studio, which helped me with my photo studio and questions, and to Aaron Gang who took the flattering photos of me.

My teachers who educated and inspired me deserve my great thanks and gratitude, especially my high school teachers who supported my talents and introduced me to jewelry-making. All of your lessons and encouragement opened my eyes to new media and the many ways to see the world around me.

This book is dedicated to all of you.